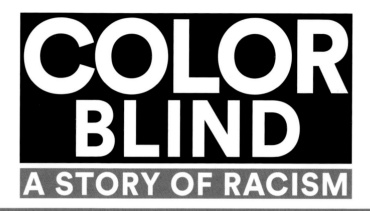

COLOR BLIND
A STORY OF RACISM

Written by **JOHNATHAN HARRIS**

Art by **DONALD HUDSON** and **GARRY LEACH**

Colors by **FAHRIZA KAMAPUTRA**

Lettering by **TYLER SMITH**
for Comicraft

Zuiker Press

Los Angeles

COLORBLIND: A STORY OF RACISM

Johnathan Harris Photographs © 2019 Johnathan Harris

Written by Anthony E. Zuiker
Art by Donald Hudson
Cover art by Garry Leach
Colors by Fahriza Kamaputra
Lettering by Tyler Smith for Comicraft
Designed by Roberta Melzl
Edited by Dave Elliott

Founders: Michelle & Anthony E. Zuiker
Publisher: David Wilk

Published by Zuiker Press
16255 Ventura Blvd.
Suite #900
Encino, CA 91436
United States of America

Visit us online at www.zuikerpress.com

ISBN 978-1-947378-12-4 (hardcover)

PRINTED IN CANADA
April 2019
10 9 8 7 6 5 4 3 2 1

DEDICATED TO... every young person who needs to be reminded they are not alone.

HOPE lies within these pages.

ZUIKER PRESS

... is a husband and wife publishing company that champions the voices of young authors. We are an **ISSUE-BASED** literary house. All of our authors have elected to tell their personal stories and be ambassadors of their cause. Their goal, as is ours, is that young people will learn from their pain and heroics and find **HOPE**, **CHANGE**, and **HAPPINESS** in their own lives.

4

TEACHER'S CORNER

SHANNON LIVELY

is a National Board Certified educator with a bachelor's degree in elementary education from the University of Nevada, Las Vegas, a master's degree from Southern Utah University, as well as advanced degrees in differentiated instruction and technology. In 2013, she was awarded the Barrick Gold One Classroom at a Time grant, and then chosen as Teacher of the Year. She is currently teaching fifth grade at John C. Vanderburg Elementary School in Henderson, Nevada.

WHY WE HONOR TEACHERS

We understand the amount of hard work, time and preparation it takes to be a teacher! At Zuiker Press, we have done the preparation for you. With each book we publish, we have created printable resources for you and your students. Our differentiated reading guides, vocabulary activities, writing prompts, extension activities, assessments, and answer keys are all available in one convenient location. Visit Zuikerpress.com, click on the For Educators tab, and access the **DOWNLOADABLE GUIDES** for teachers. These PDFs include everything you need to print and go! Each lesson is designed to cover Common Core standards for many subjects across the curriculum. We hope these resources help teachers utilize each story to the fullest extent!

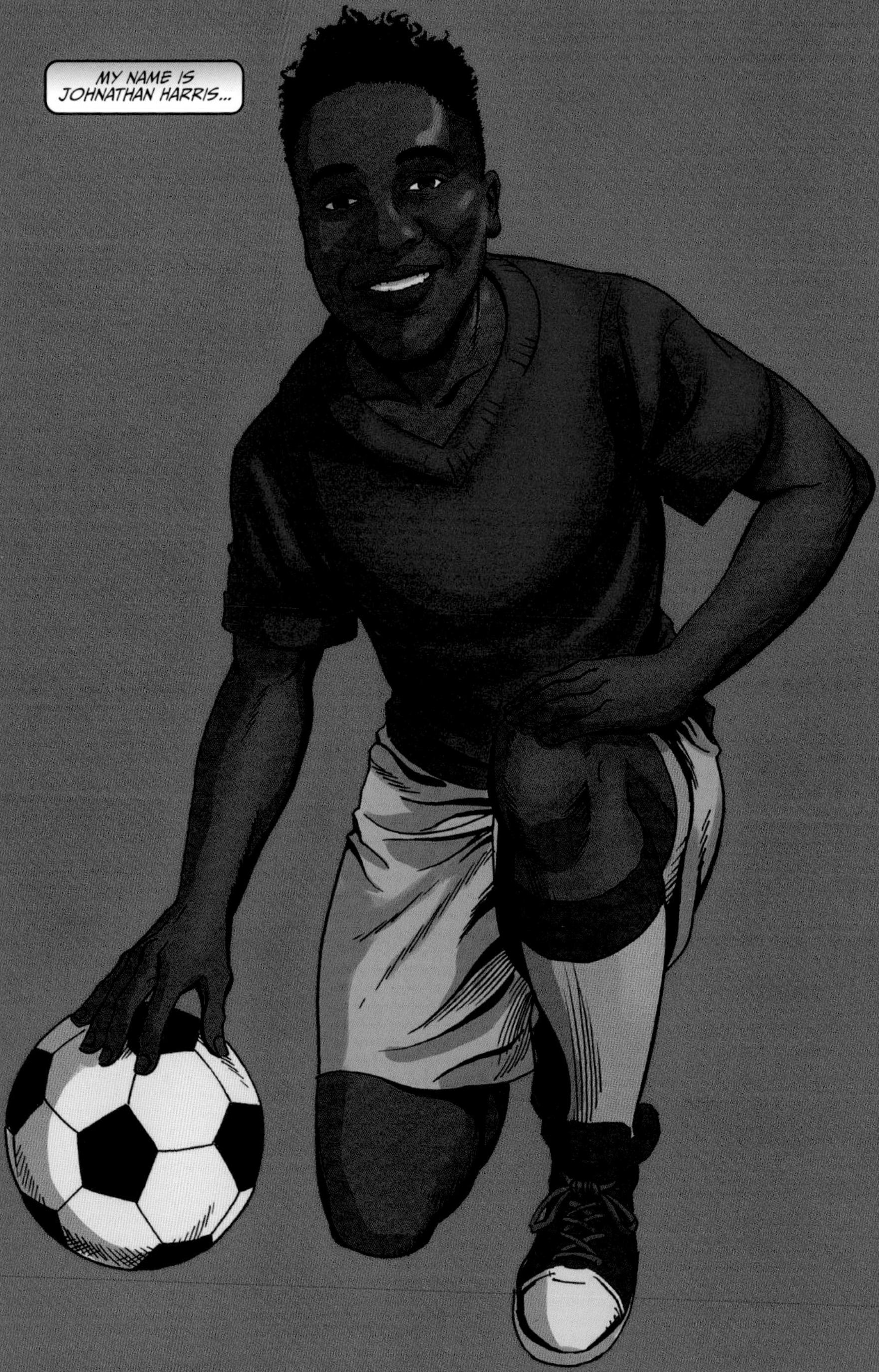
MY NAME IS JOHNATHAN HARRIS...

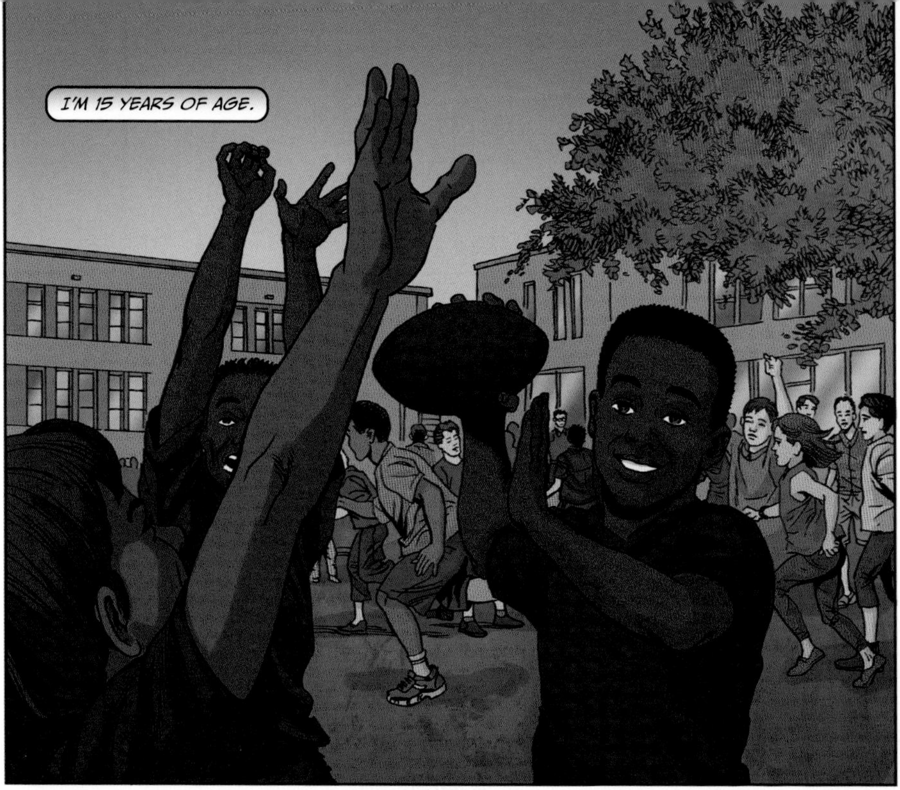
I'M 15 YEARS OF AGE.

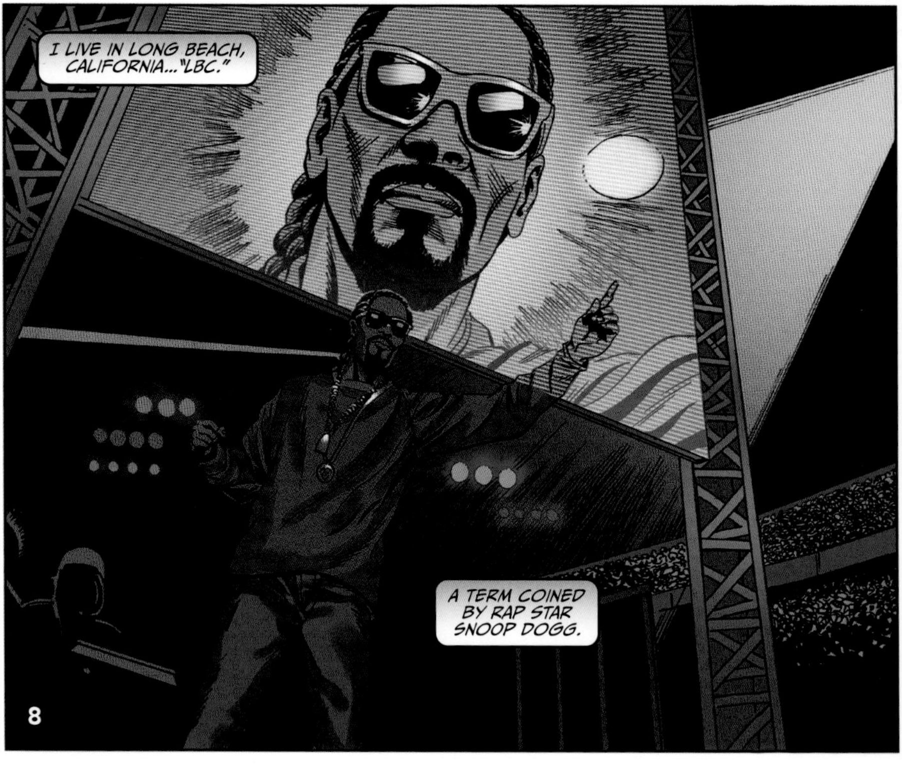
I LIVE IN LONG BEACH, CALIFORNIA..."LBC."
A TERM COINED BY RAP STAR SNOOP DOGG.

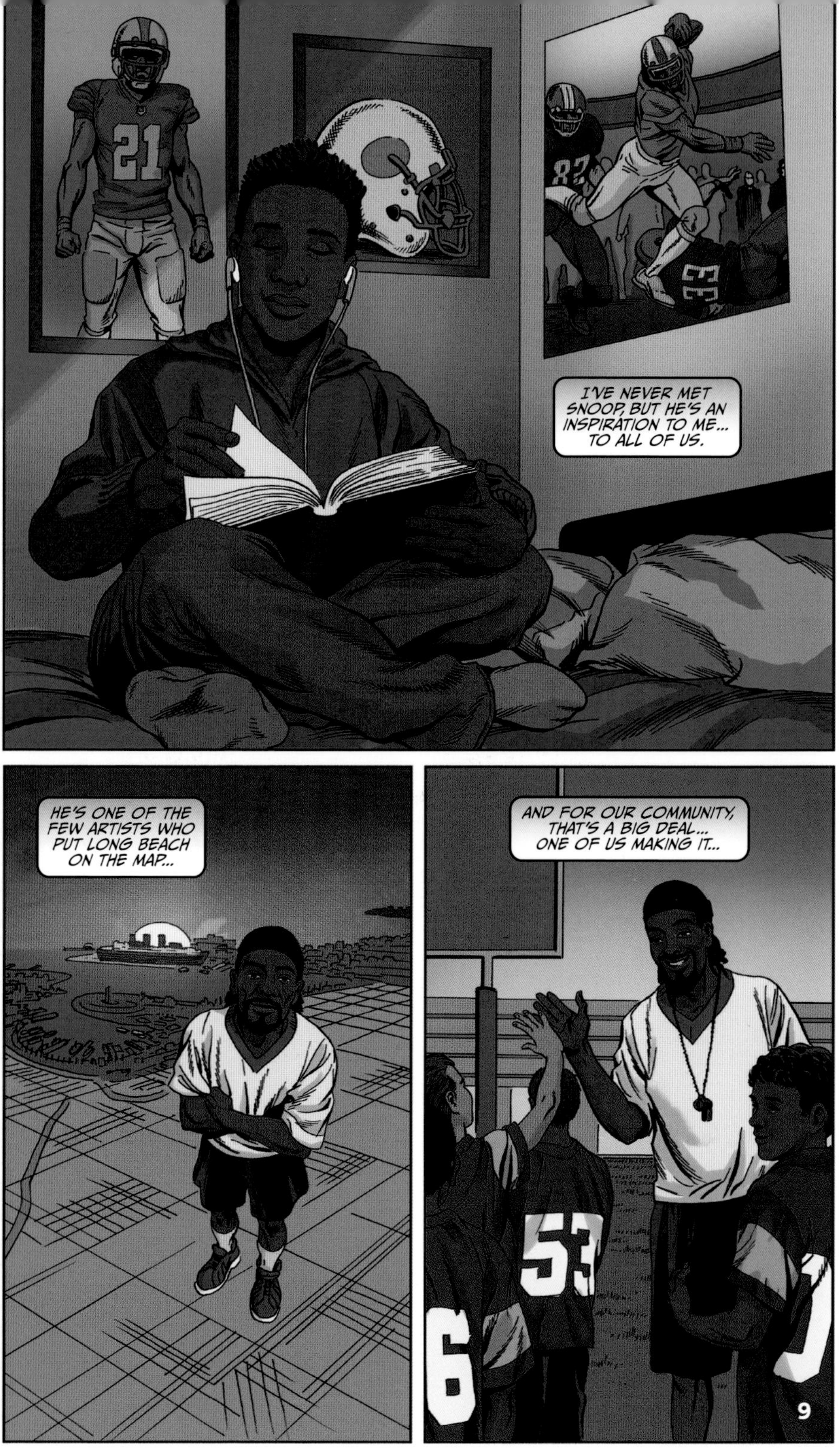
I'VE NEVER MET SNOOP, BUT HE'S AN INSPIRATION TO ME... TO ALL OF US.
HE'S ONE OF THE FEW ARTISTS WHO PUT LONG BEACH ON THE MAP...
AND FOR OUR COMMUNITY, THAT'S A BIG DEAL... ONE OF US MAKING IT...

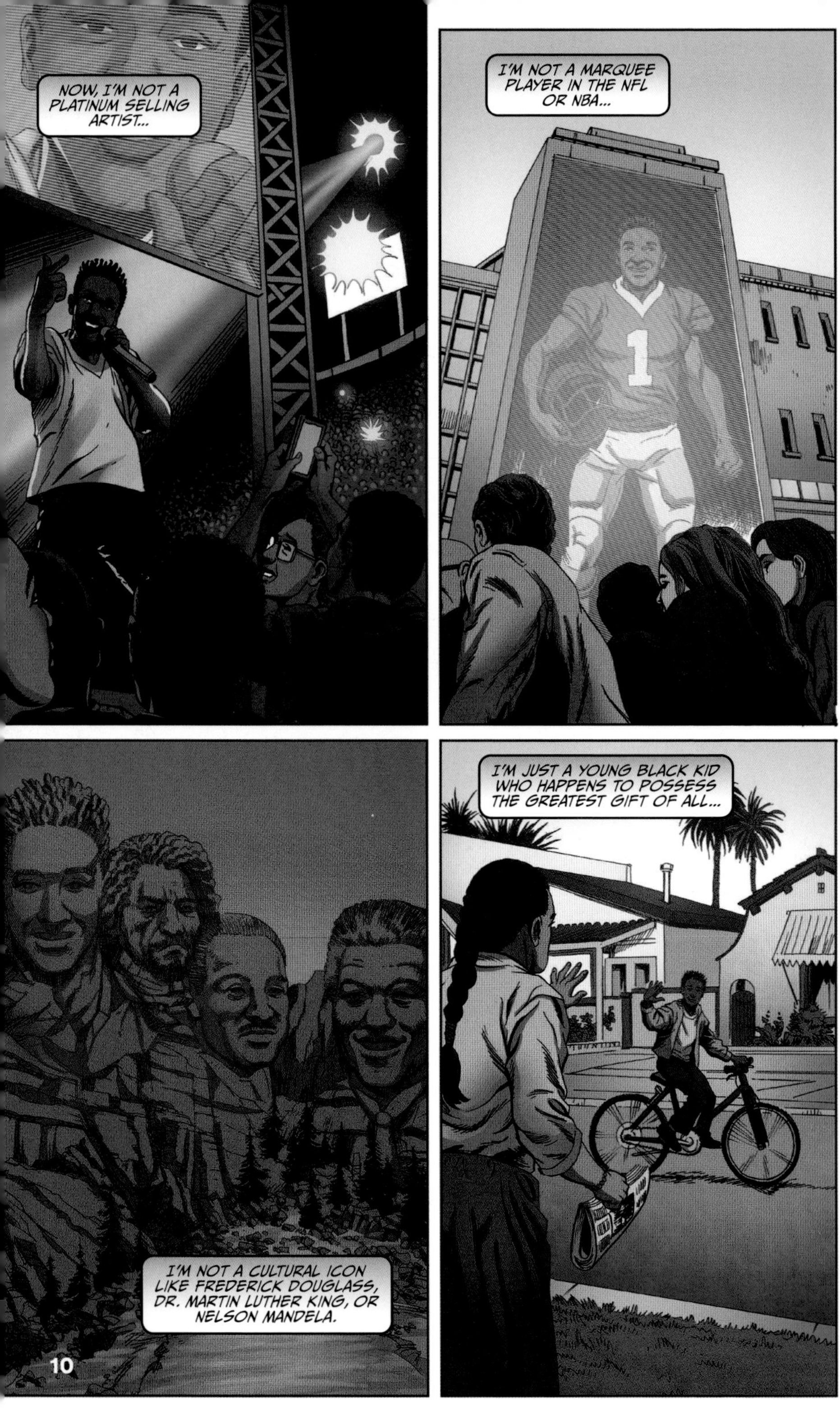
NOW, I'M NOT A PLATINUM SELLING ARTIST...
I'M NOT A MARQUEE PLAYER IN THE NFL OR NBA...
I'M NOT A CULTURAL ICON LIKE FREDERICK DOUGLASS, DR. MARTIN LUTHER KING, OR NELSON MANDELA.
I'M JUST A YOUNG BLACK KID WHO HAPPENS TO POSSESS THE GREATEST GIFT OF ALL...

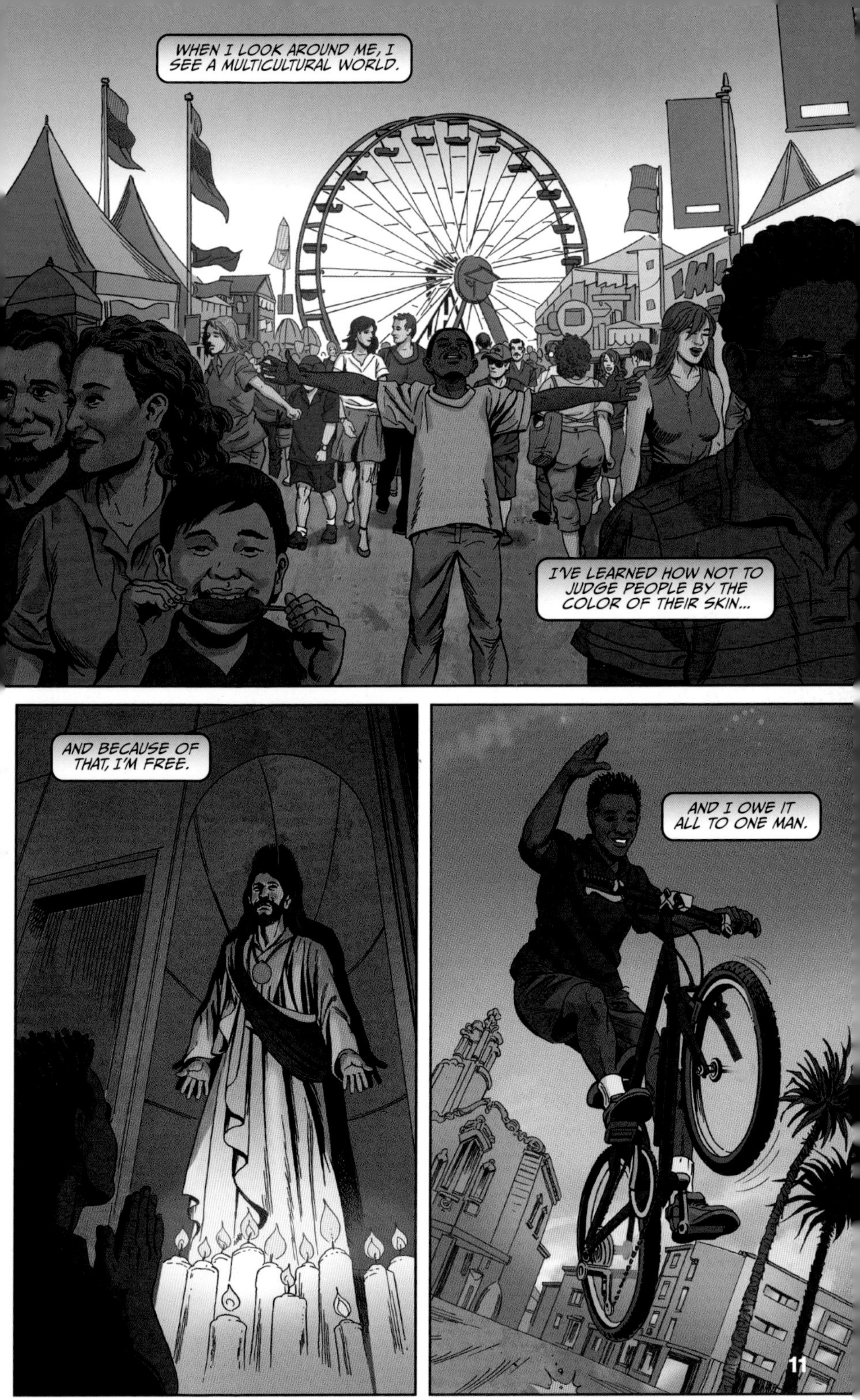
WHEN I LOOK AROUND ME, I SEE A MULTICULTURAL WORLD.
I'VE LEARNED HOW NOT TO JUDGE PEOPLE BY THE COLOR OF THEIR SKIN...
AND BECAUSE OF THAT, I'M FREE.
AND I OWE IT ALL TO ONE MAN.

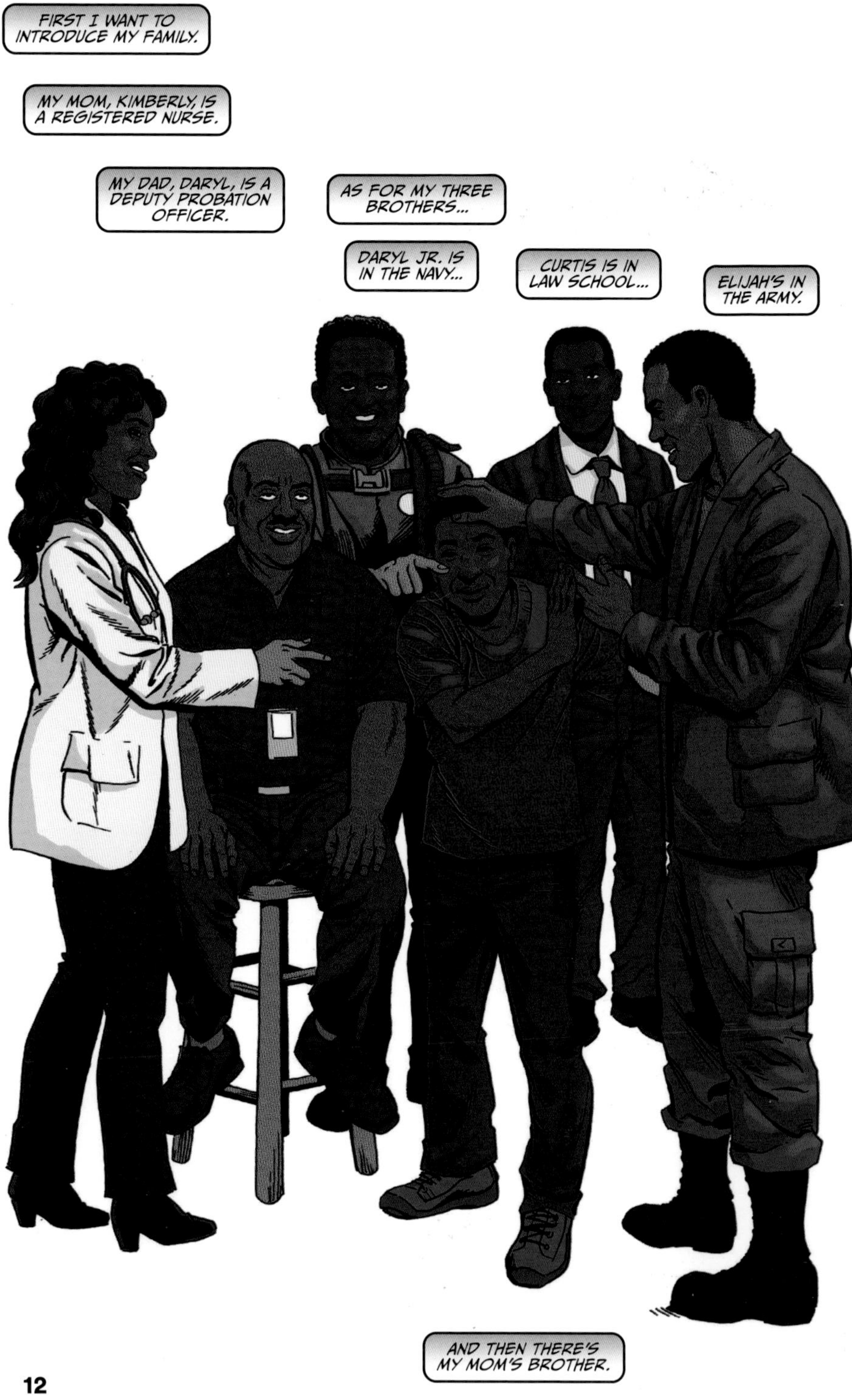
FIRST I WANT TO INTRODUCE MY FAMILY.
MY MOM, KIMBERLY, IS A REGISTERED NURSE.
MY DAD, DARYL, IS A DEPUTY PROBATION OFFICER.
AS FOR MY THREE BROTHERS...
DARYL JR. IS IN THE NAVY...
CURTIS IS IN LAW SCHOOL...
ELIJAH'S IN THE ARMY.
AND THEN THERE'S MY MOM'S BROTHER.

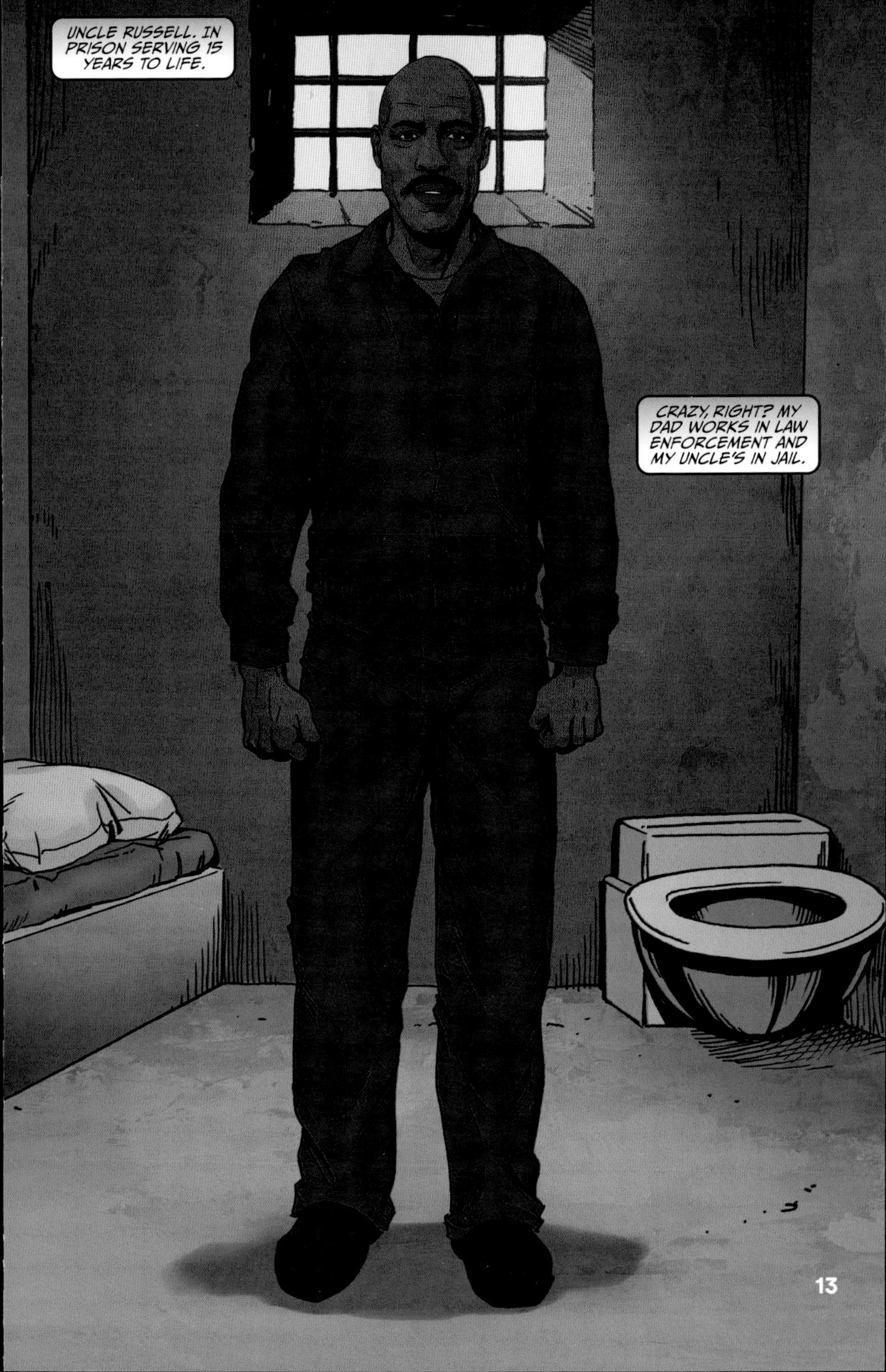
UNCLE RUSSELL. IN PRISON SERVING 15 YEARS TO LIFE.
CRAZY, RIGHT? MY DAD WORKS IN LAW ENFORCEMENT AND MY UNCLE'S IN JAIL.

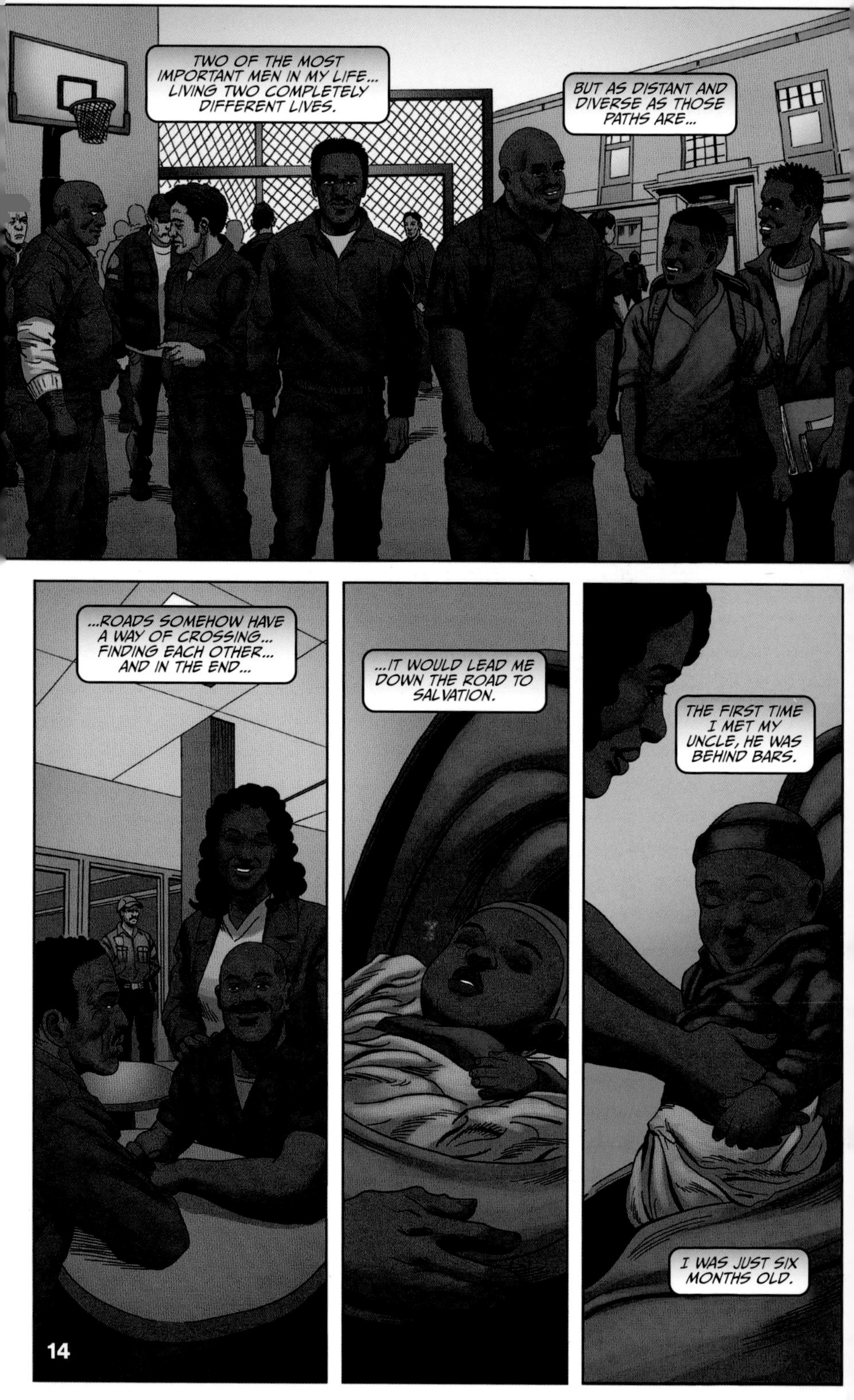
TWO OF THE MOST IMPORTANT MEN IN MY LIFE... LIVING TWO COMPLETELY DIFFERENT LIVES.
BUT AS DISTANT AND DIVERSE AS THOSE PATHS ARE...
...ROADS SOMEHOW HAVE A WAY OF CROSSING... FINDING EACH OTHER... AND IN THE END...
...IT WOULD LEAD ME DOWN THE ROAD TO SALVATION.
THE FIRST TIME I MET MY UNCLE, HE WAS BEHIND BARS.
I WAS JUST SIX MONTHS OLD.

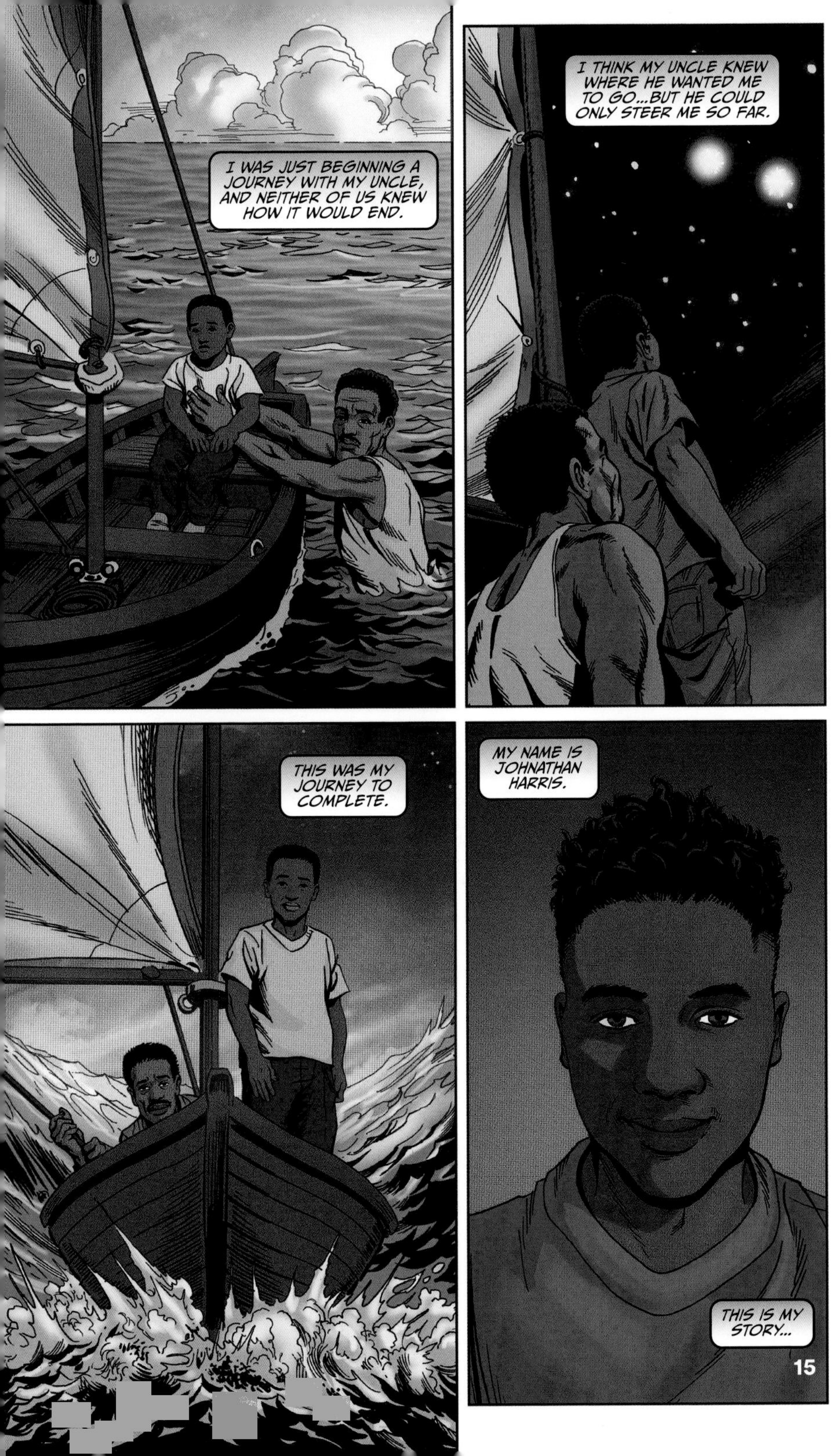
I WAS JUST BEGINNING A JOURNEY WITH MY UNCLE, AND NEITHER OF US KNEW HOW IT WOULD END.
I THINK MY UNCLE KNEW WHERE HE WANTED ME TO GO...BUT HE COULD ONLY STEER ME SO FAR.
THIS WAS MY JOURNEY TO COMPLETE.
MY NAME IS JOHNATHAN HARRIS.
THIS IS MY STORY...

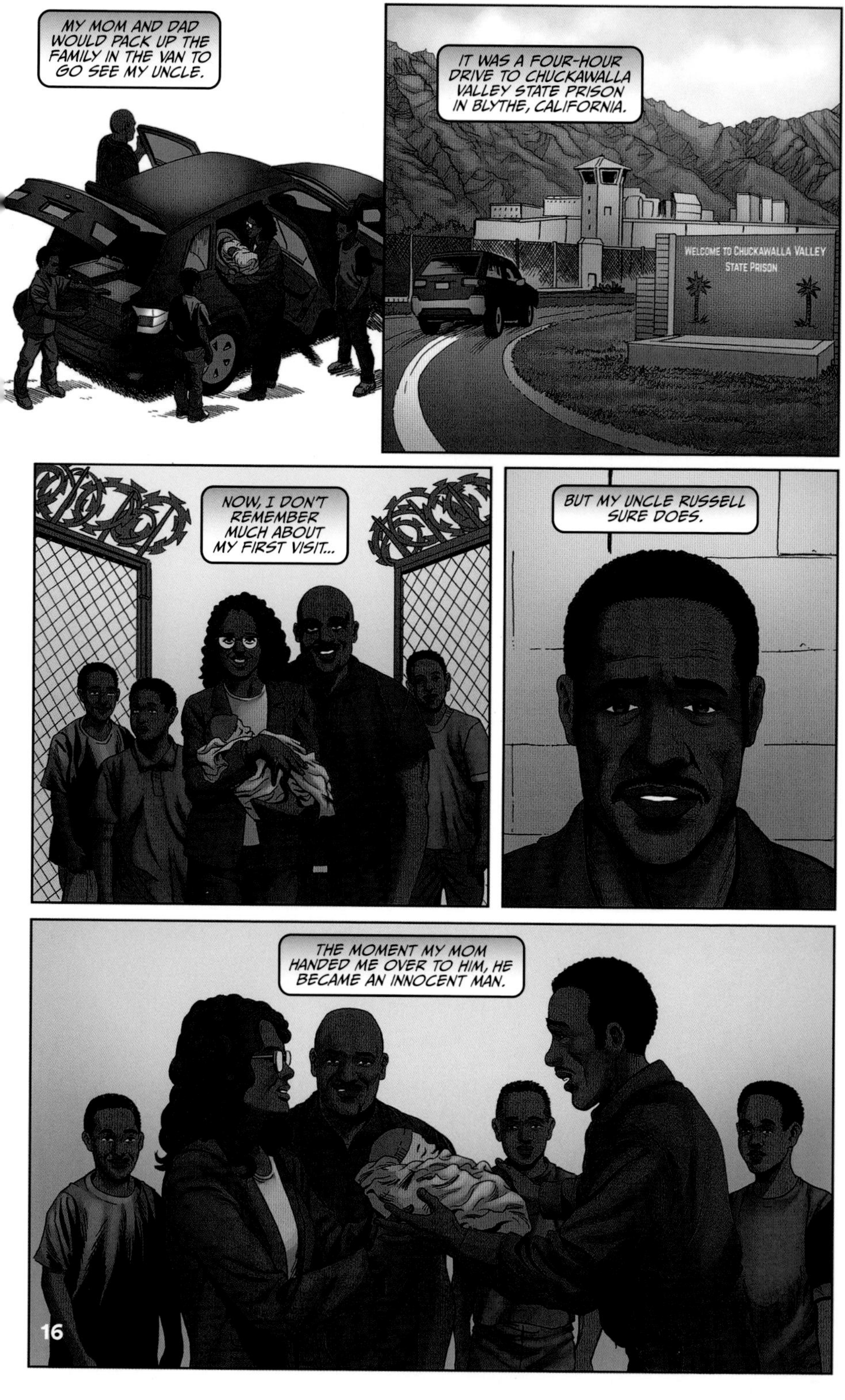
MY MOM AND DAD WOULD PACK UP THE FAMILY IN THE VAN TO GO SEE MY UNCLE.
IT WAS A FOUR-HOUR DRIVE TO CHUCKAWALLA VALLEY STATE PRISON IN BLYTHE, CALIFORNIA.
WELCOME TO CHUCKAWALLA VALLEY STATE PRISON
NOW, I DON'T REMEMBER MUCH ABOUT MY FIRST VISIT...
BUT MY UNCLE RUSSELL SURE DOES.
THE MOMENT MY MOM HANDED ME OVER TO HIM, HE BECAME AN INNOCENT MAN.

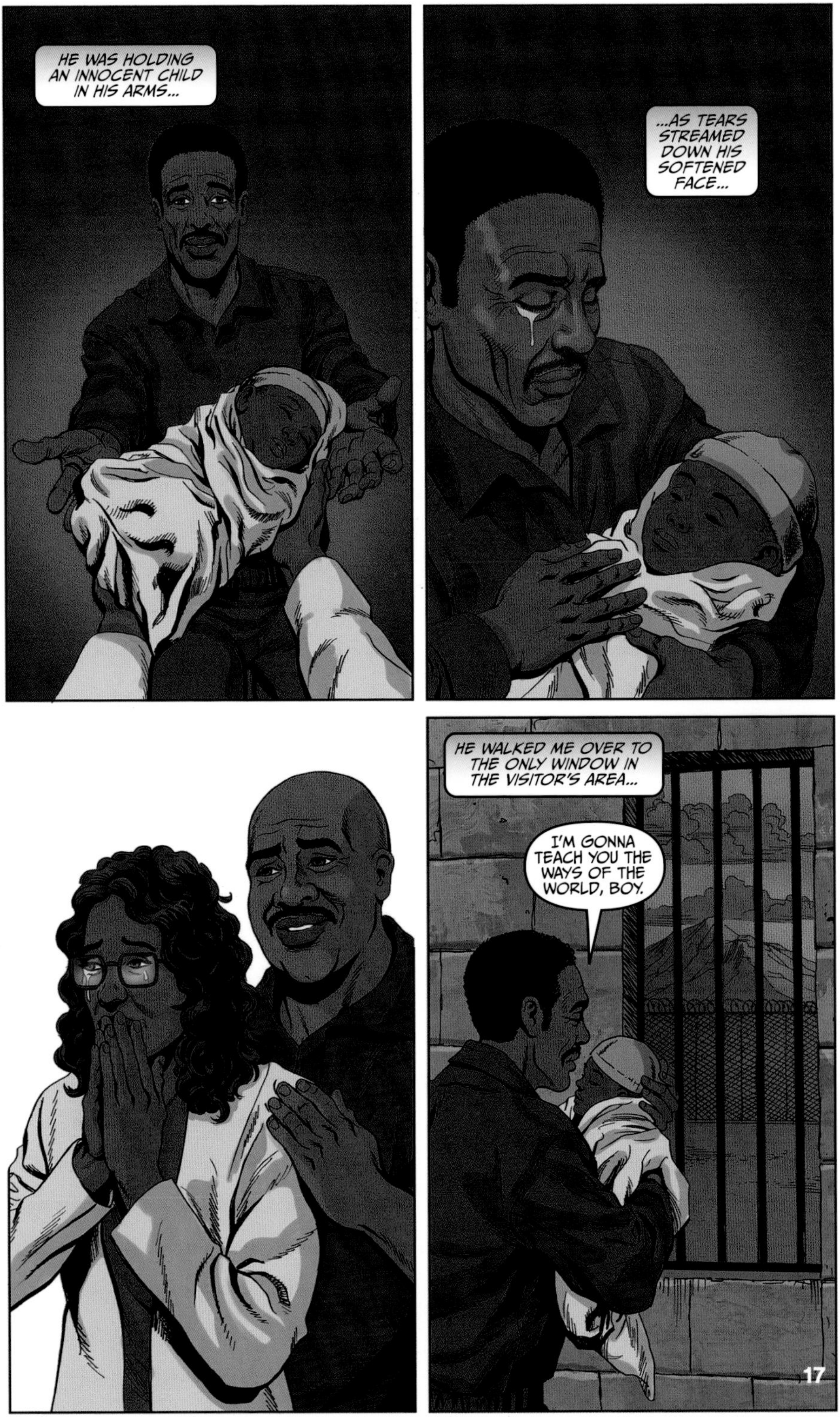
HE WAS HOLDING AN INNOCENT CHILD IN HIS ARMS...
...AS TEARS STREAMED DOWN HIS SOFTENED FACE...
HE WALKED ME OVER TO THE ONLY WINDOW IN THE VISITOR'S AREA...
I'M GONNA TEACH YOU THE WAYS OF THE WORLD, BOY.

YOU ARE MY HEART... YOU ARE MY SOUL... YOU ARE MY SALVATION... AND WHILE I'M INSIDE, LORD AS MY WITNESS, I'M GONNA MAKE SURE YOU'RE OKAY ON THE OUTSIDE.

AND WITH THOSE WORDS, UNCLE RUSSELL ROCKED ME GENTLY ASLEEP.

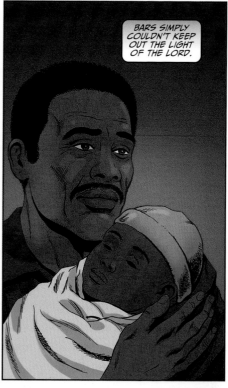

BARS SIMPLY COULDN'T KEEP OUT THE LIGHT OF THE LORD.

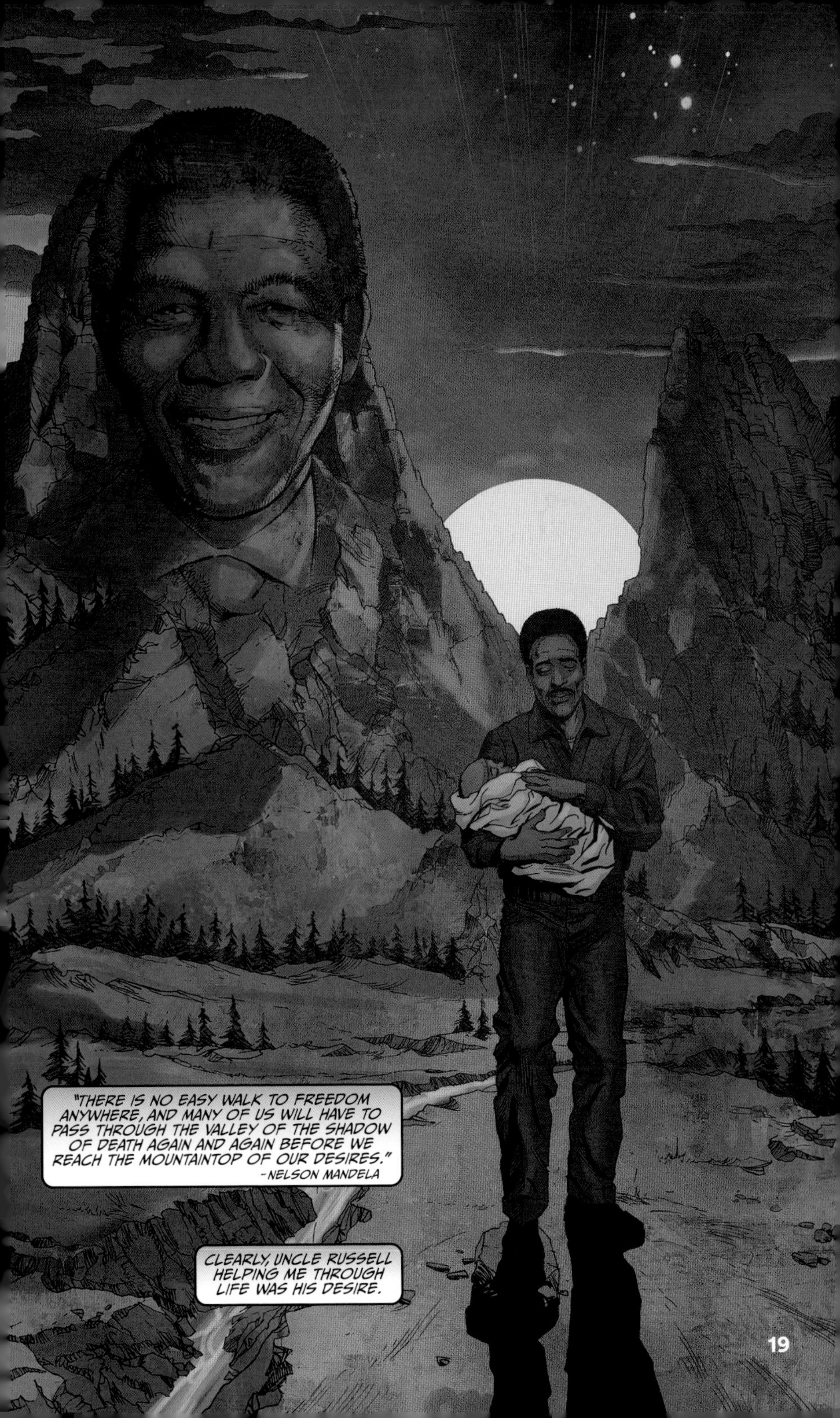
"THERE IS NO EASY WALK TO FREEDOM ANYWHERE, AND MANY OF US WILL HAVE TO PASS THROUGH THE VALLEY OF THE SHADOW OF DEATH AGAIN AND AGAIN BEFORE WE REACH THE MOUNTAINTOP OF OUR DESIRES." -NELSON MANDELA
CLEARLY, UNCLE RUSSELL HELPING ME THROUGH LIFE WAS HIS DESIRE.

WHAT I DIDN'T KNOW UNTIL MUCH LATER...

...IS THAT MY DESIRE TO LIVE MY LIFE UNDER HIS GUIDANCE WOULD ULTIMATELY BRING US CLOSER TOGETHER...

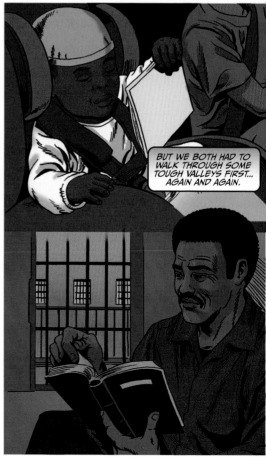

BUT WE BOTH HAD TO WALK THROUGH SOME TOUGH VALLEYS FIRST... AGAIN AND AGAIN.

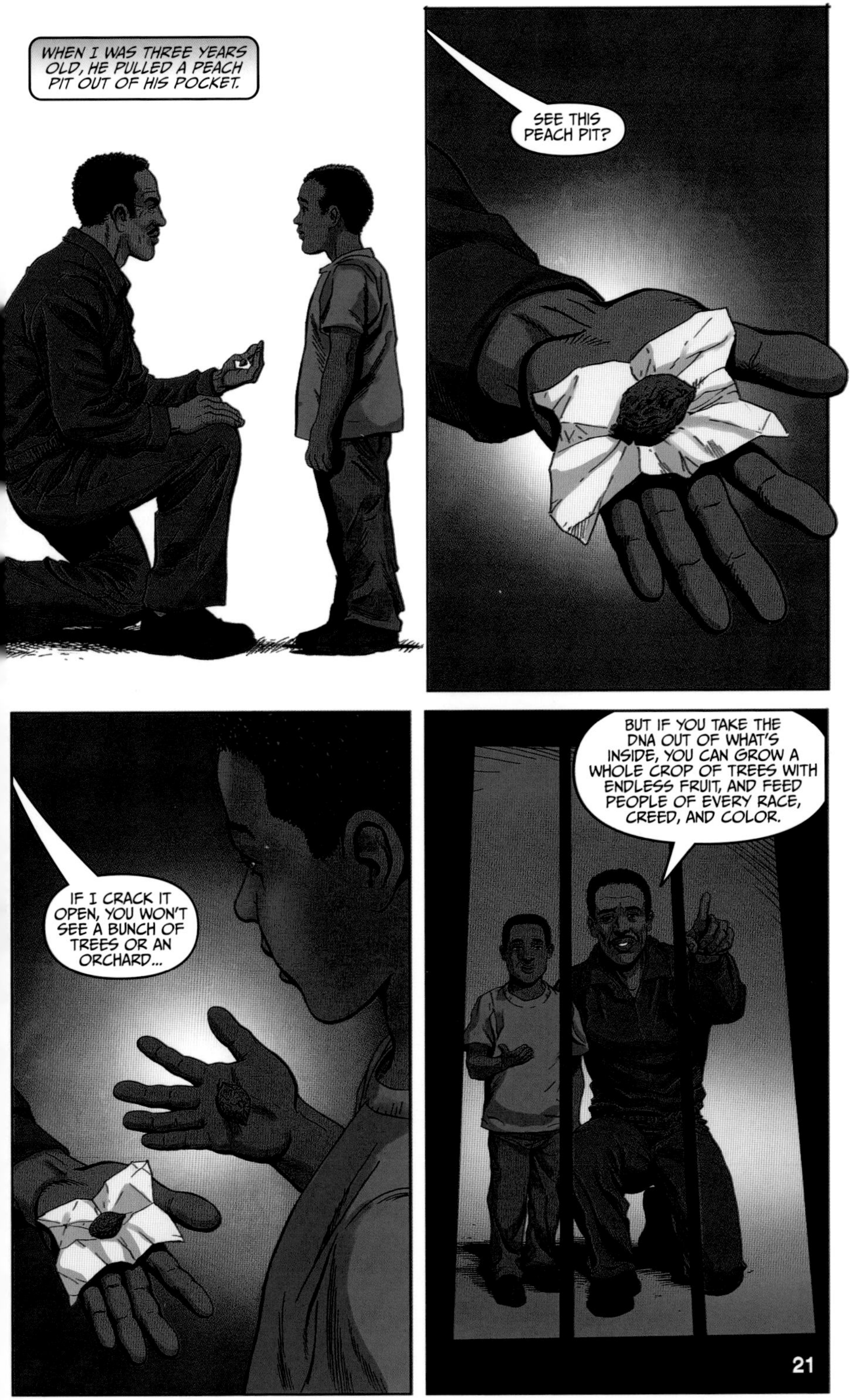
WHEN I WAS THREE YEARS OLD, HE PULLED A PEACH PIT OUT OF HIS POCKET.
SEE THIS PEACH PIT?
IF I CRACK IT OPEN, YOU WON'T SEE A BUNCH OF TREES OR AN ORCHARD...
BUT IF YOU TAKE THE DNA OUT OF WHAT'S INSIDE, YOU CAN GROW A WHOLE CROP OF TREES WITH ENDLESS FRUIT, AND FEED PEOPLE OF EVERY RACE, CREED, AND COLOR.

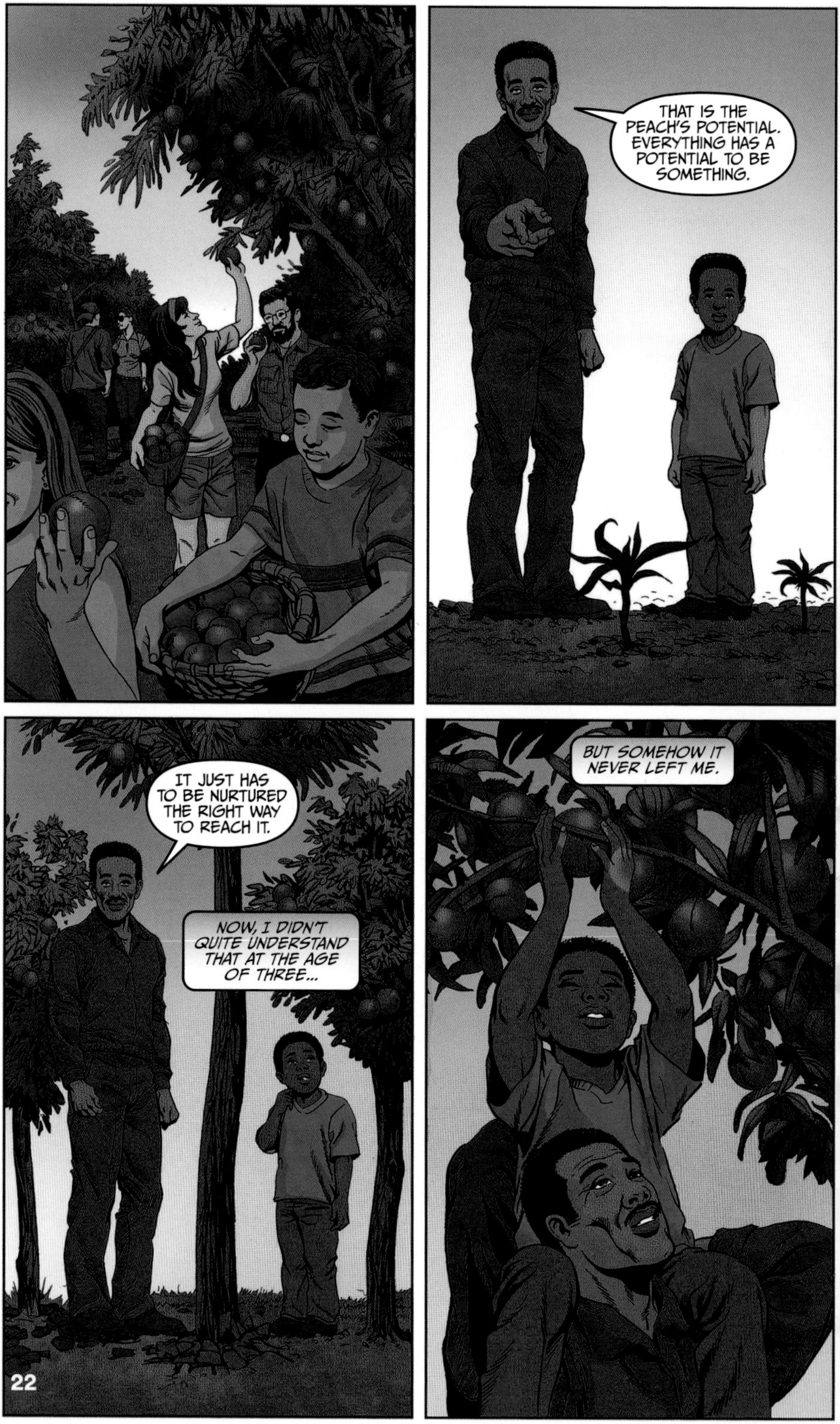
THAT IS THE PEACH'S POTENTIAL. EVERYTHING HAS A POTENTIAL TO BE SOMETHING.
IT JUST HAS TO BE NURTURED THE RIGHT WAY TO REACH IT.
NOW, I DIDN'T QUITE UNDERSTAND THAT AT THE AGE OF THREE...
BUT SOMEHOW IT NEVER LEFT ME.

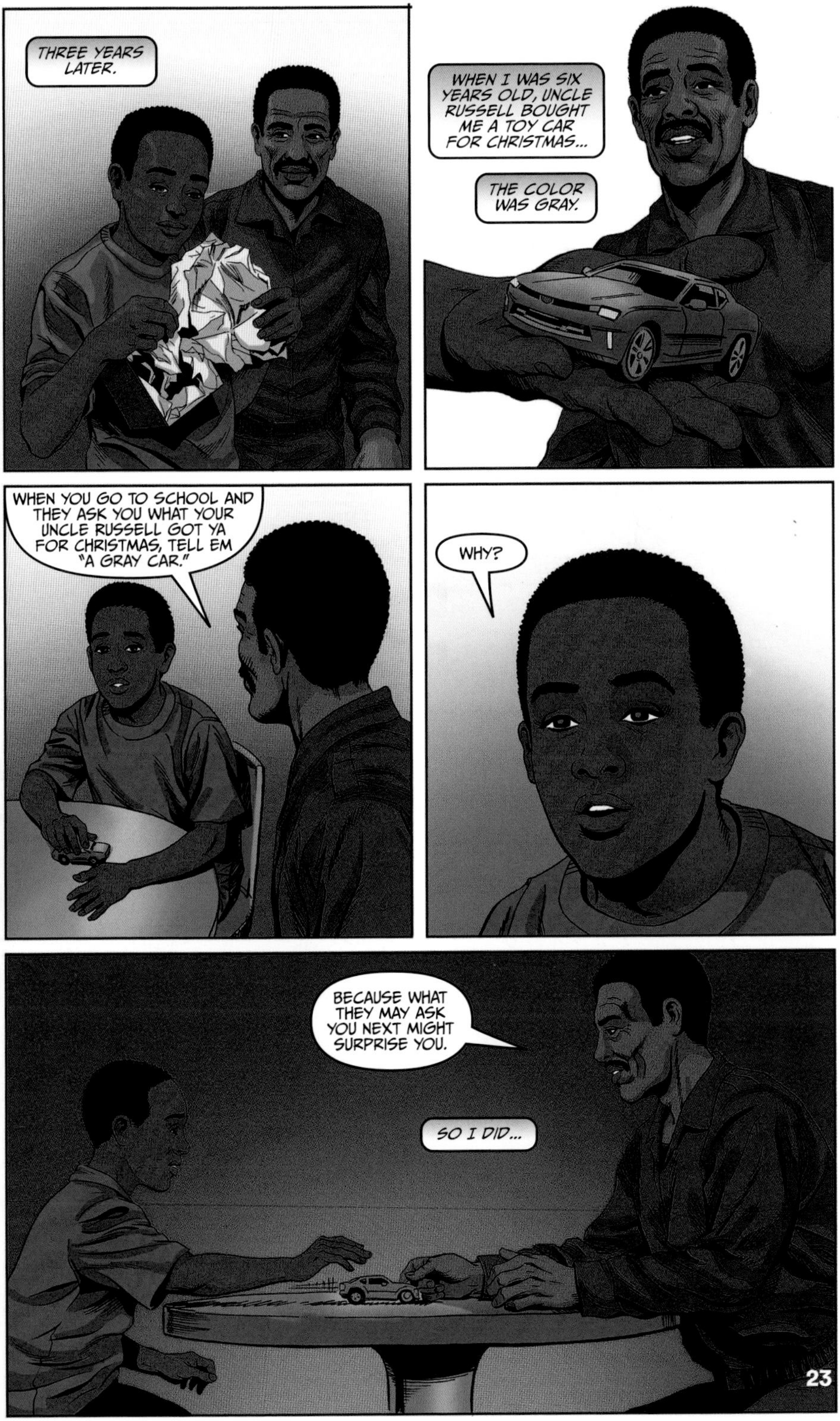
THREE YEARS LATER.
WHEN I WAS SIX YEARS OLD, UNCLE RUSSELL BOUGHT ME A TOY CAR FOR CHRISTMAS...
THE COLOR WAS GRAY.
WHEN YOU GO TO SCHOOL AND THEY ASK YOU WHAT YOUR UNCLE RUSSELL GOT YA FOR CHRISTMAS, TELL EM "A GRAY CAR."
WHY?
BECAUSE WHAT THEY MAY ASK YOU NEXT MIGHT SURPRISE YOU.
SO I DID...

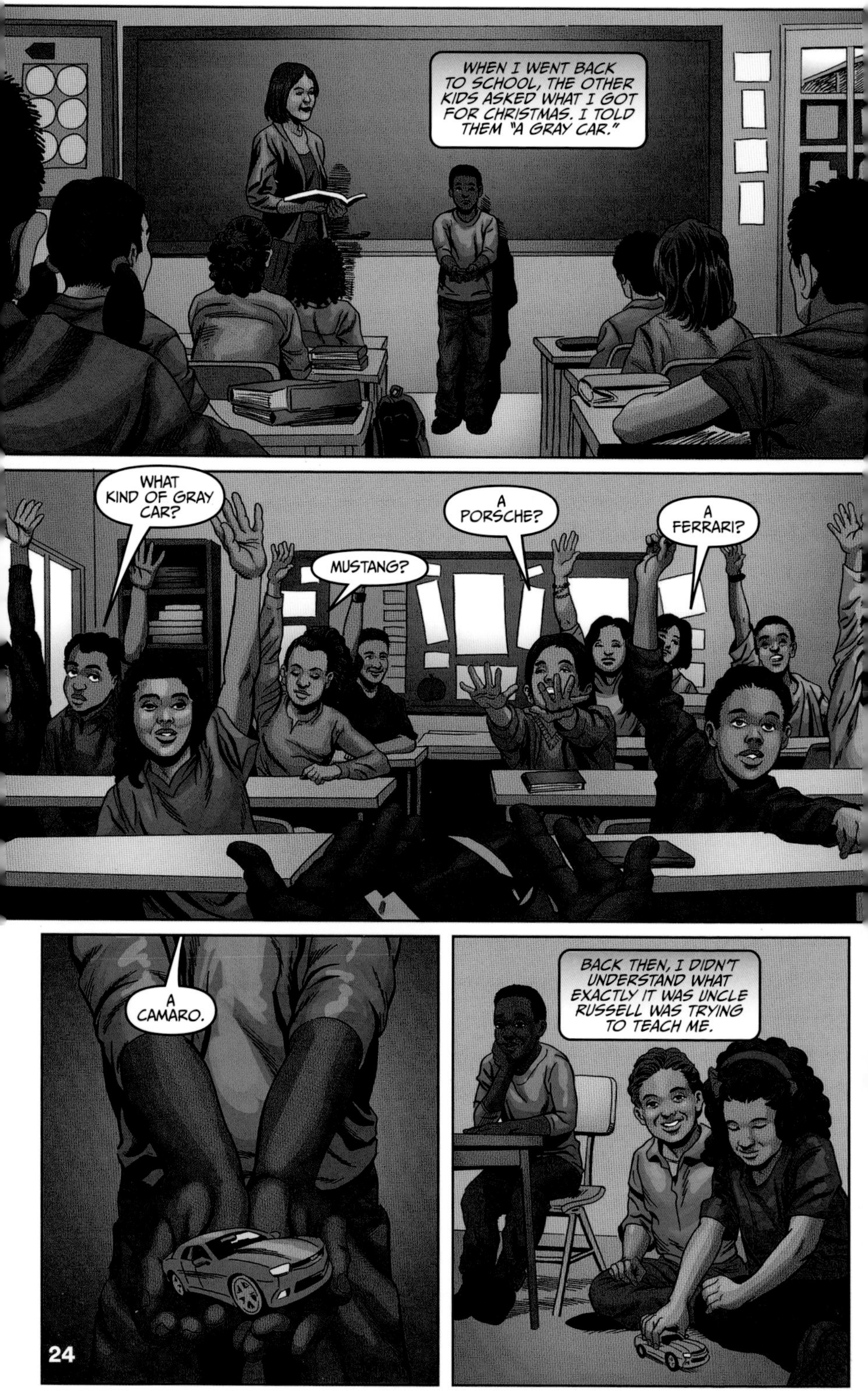

WHEN I WENT BACK TO SCHOOL, THE OTHER KIDS ASKED WHAT I GOT FOR CHRISTMAS. I TOLD THEM "A GRAY CAR."
WHAT KIND OF GRAY CAR?
MUSTANG?
A PORSCHE?
A FERRARI?
A CAMARO.
BACK THEN, I DIDN'T UNDERSTAND WHAT EXACTLY IT WAS UNCLE RUSSELL WAS TRYING TO TEACH ME.

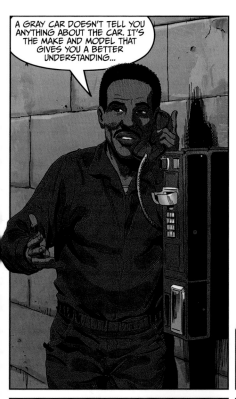

A GRAY CAR DOESN'T TELL YOU ANYTHING ABOUT THE CAR. IT'S THE MAKE AND MODEL THAT GIVES YOU A BETTER UNDERSTANDING...

THINK ABOUT CAR COLOR... LIKE YOU WOULD BODY COLOR.

WHAT UNCLE RUSSELL WAS SAYING WAS THAT JUDGING PEOPLE BY THE COLOR OF THEIR SKIN WASN'T TELLING ME ANYTHING ABOUT THEM...

IT'S ONE'S CULTURE THAT TELLS US EVERYTHING.

CULTURE IS WHERE WE TRULY STAND TOGETHER.

UNDERSTANDING ANOTHER'S CULTURE IS THE BEGINNING OF CONNECTION, AND ACCEPTANCE.

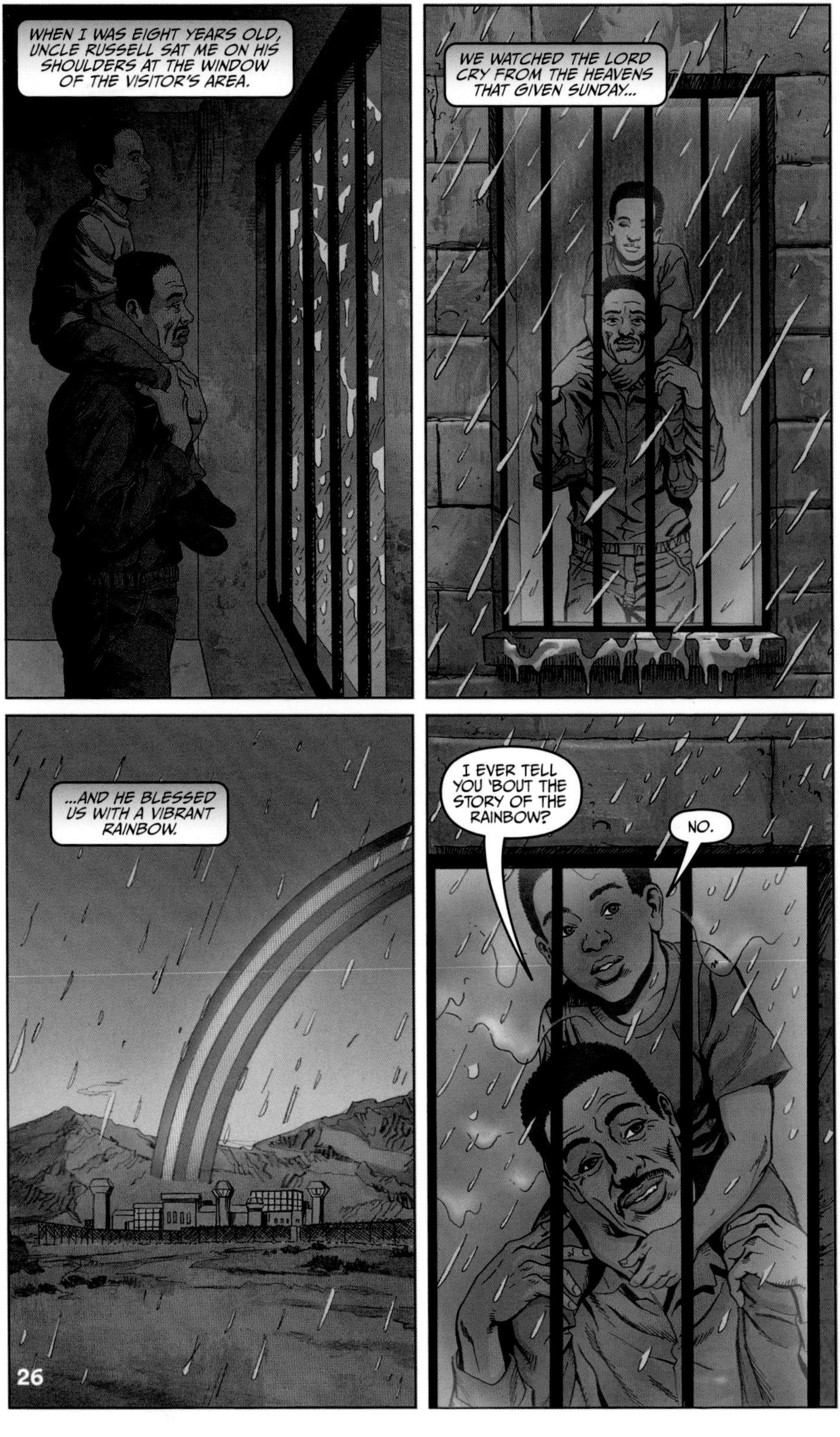
WHEN I WAS EIGHT YEARS OLD, UNCLE RUSSELL SAT ME ON HIS SHOULDERS AT THE WINDOW OF THE VISITOR'S AREA.
WE WATCHED THE LORD CRY FROM THE HEAVENS THAT GIVEN SUNDAY...
...AND HE BLESSED US WITH A VIBRANT RAINBOW.
I EVER TELL YOU 'BOUT THE STORY OF THE RAINBOW?
NO.

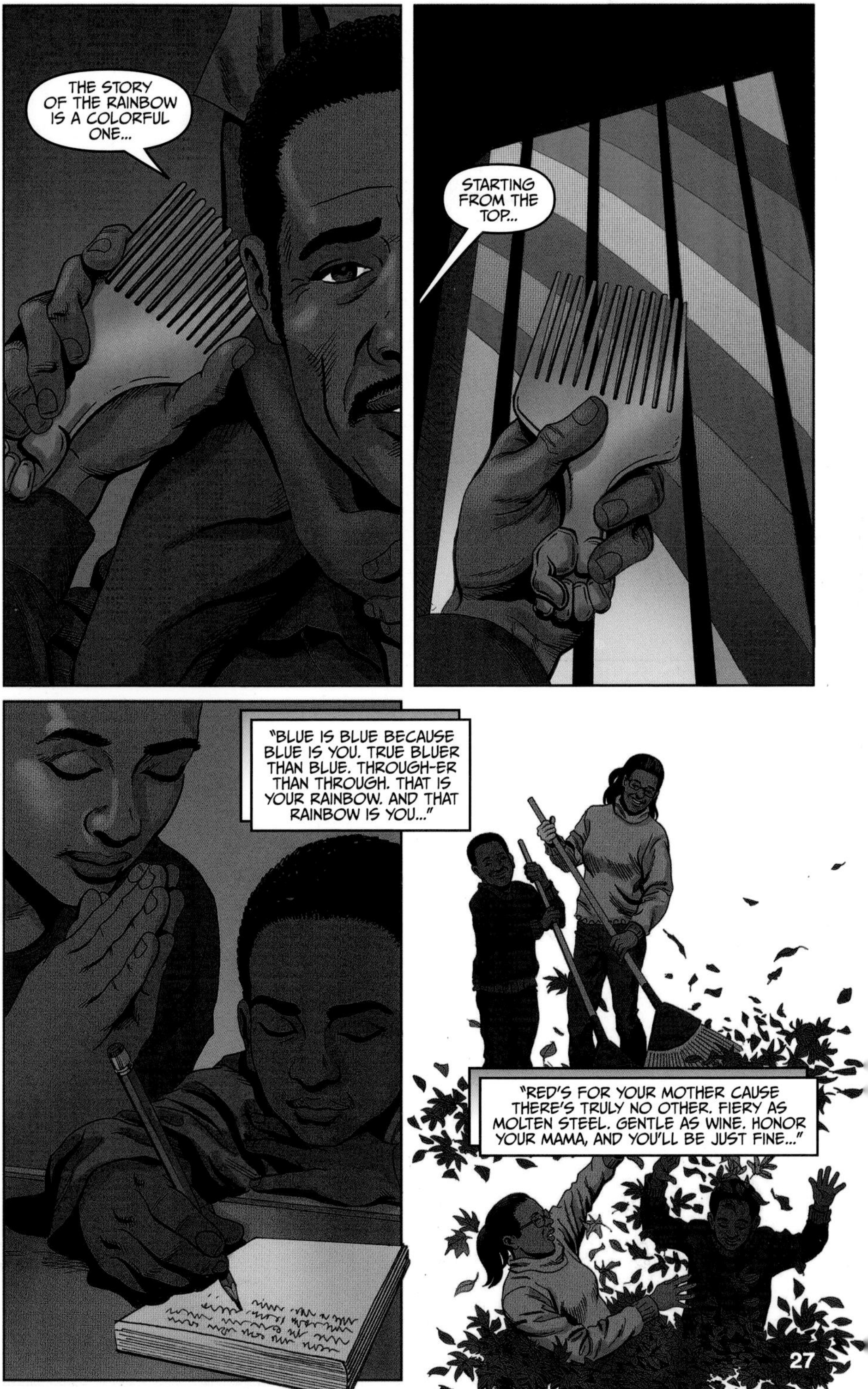
THE STORY OF THE RAINBOW IS A COLORFUL ONE...
STARTING FROM THE TOP...
"BLUE IS BLUE BECAUSE BLUE IS YOU. TRUE BLUER THAN BLUE. THROUGH-ER THAN THROUGH. THAT IS YOUR RAINBOW. AND THAT RAINBOW IS YOU..."
"RED'S FOR YOUR MOTHER CAUSE THERE'S TRULY NO OTHER. FIERY AS MOLTEN STEEL. GENTLE AS WINE. HONOR YOUR MAMA, AND YOU'LL BE JUST FINE..."

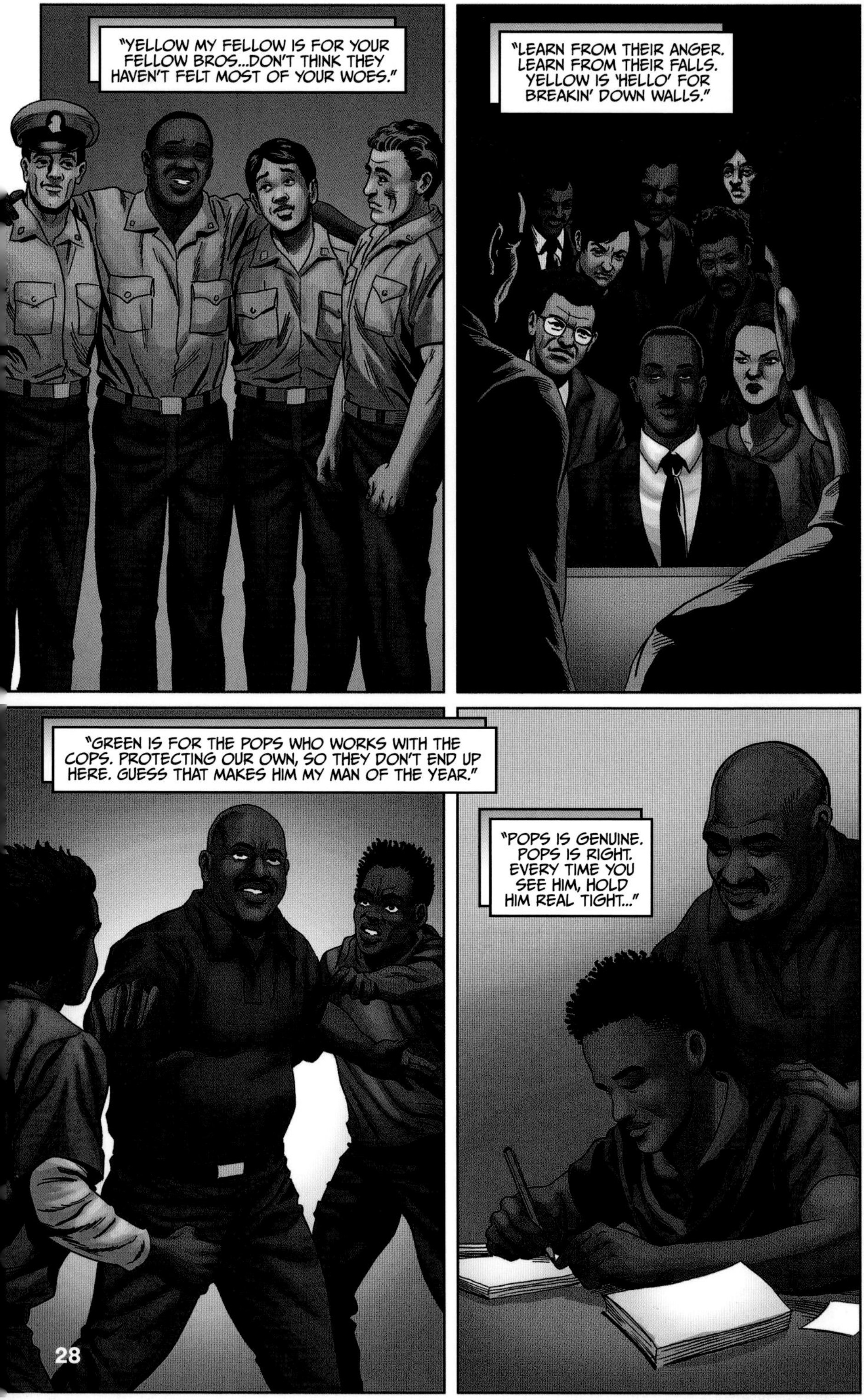
"YELLOW MY FELLOW IS FOR YOUR FELLOW BROS...DON'T THINK THEY HAVEN'T FELT MOST OF YOUR WOES."
"LEARN FROM THEIR ANGER. LEARN FROM THEIR FALLS. YELLOW IS 'HELLO' FOR BREAKIN' DOWN WALLS."
"GREEN IS FOR THE POPS WHO WORKS WITH THE COPS. PROTECTING OUR OWN, SO THEY DON'T END UP HERE. GUESS THAT MAKES HIM MY MAN OF THE YEAR."
"POPS IS GENUINE. POPS IS RIGHT. EVERY TIME YOU SEE HIM, HOLD HIM REAL TIGHT..."

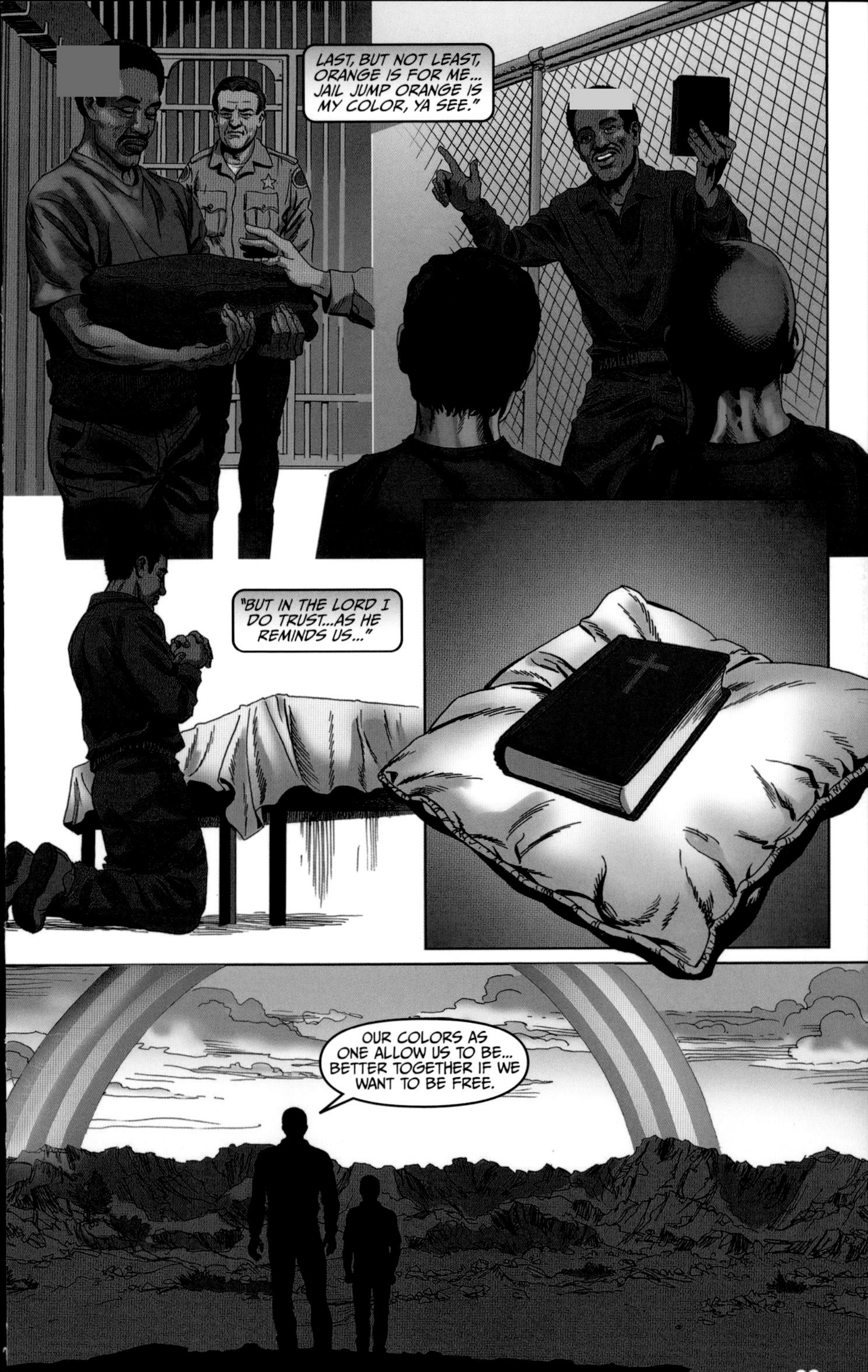

LAST, BUT NOT LEAST, ORANGE IS FOR ME... JAIL JUMP ORANGE IS MY COLOR, YA SEE."
"BUT IN THE LORD I DO TRUST...AS HE REMINDS US..."
OUR COLORS AS ONE ALLOW US TO BE... BETTER TOGETHER IF WE WANT TO BE FREE.

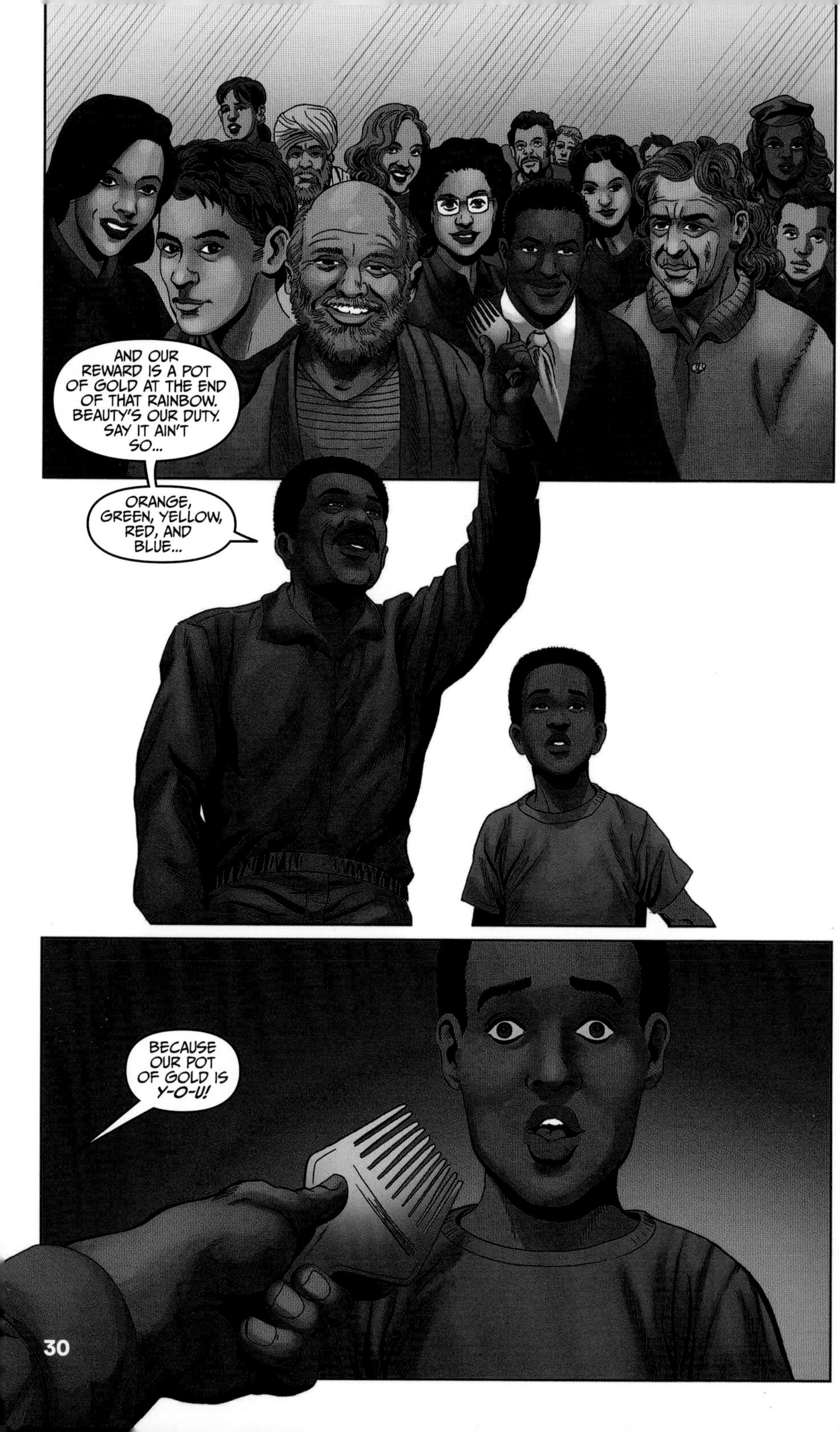
AND OUR REWARD IS A POT OF GOLD AT THE END OF THAT RAINBOW. BEAUTY'S OUR DUTY. SAY IT AIN'T SO...
ORANGE, GREEN, YELLOW, RED, AND BLUE...
BECAUSE OUR POT OF GOLD IS Y-O-U!

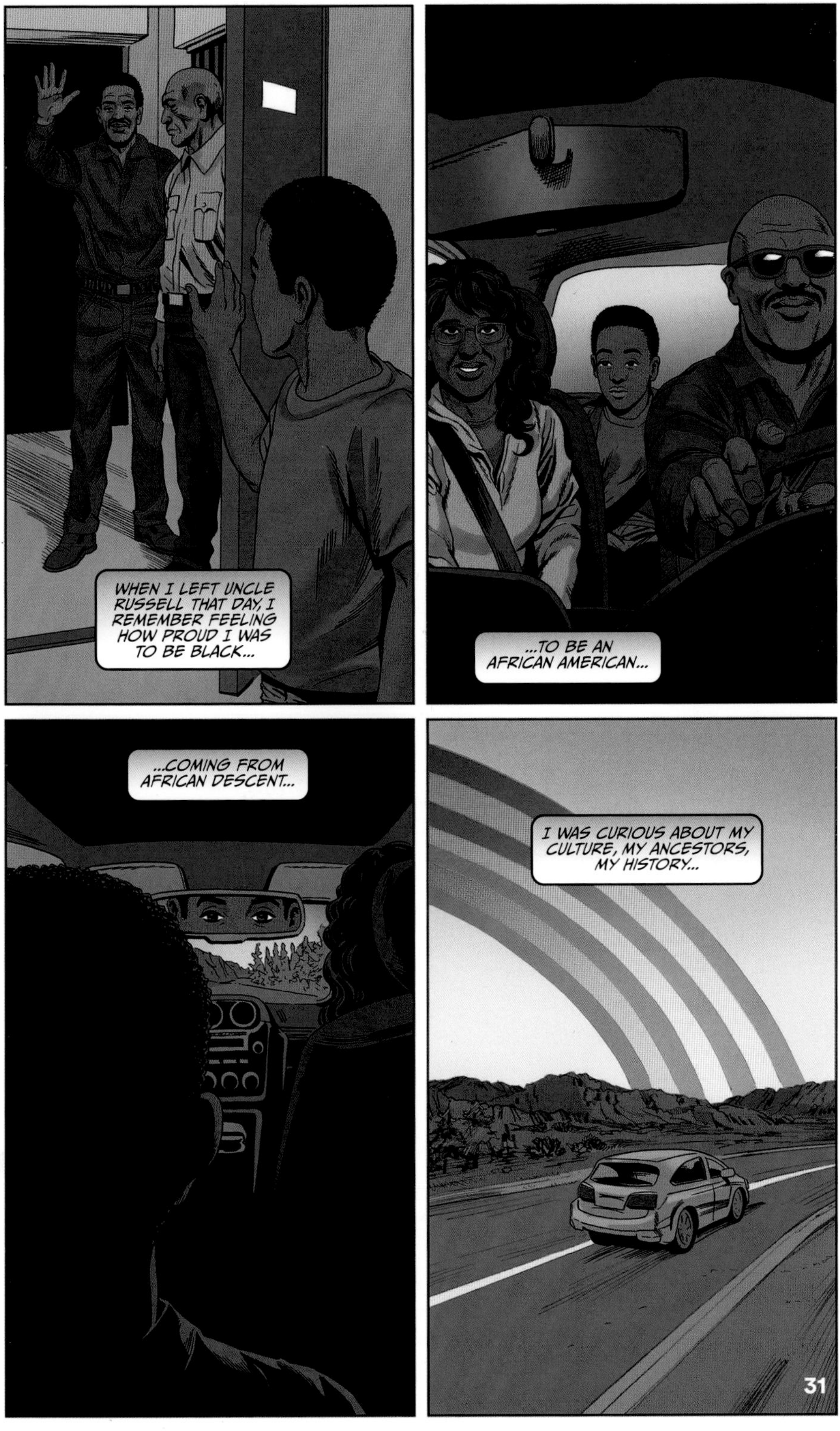
WHEN I LEFT UNCLE RUSSELL THAT DAY, I REMEMBER FEELING HOW PROUD I WAS TO BE BLACK...
...TO BE AN AFRICAN AMERICAN...
...COMING FROM AFRICAN DESCENT...
I WAS CURIOUS ABOUT MY CULTURE, MY ANCESTORS, MY HISTORY...

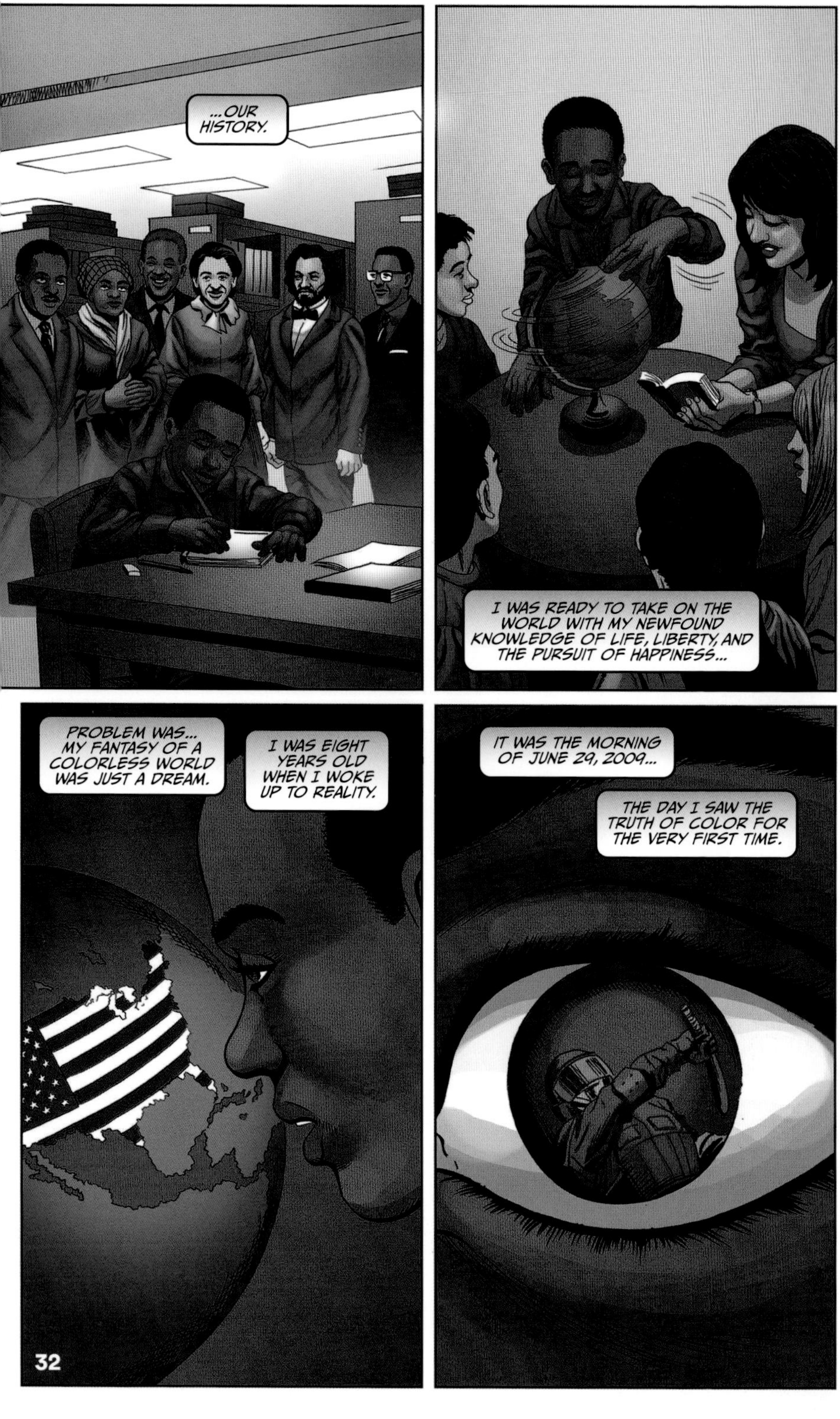
...OUR HISTORY.
I WAS READY TO TAKE ON THE WORLD WITH MY NEWFOUND KNOWLEDGE OF LIFE, LIBERTY, AND THE PURSUIT OF HAPPINESS...
PROBLEM WAS... MY FANTASY OF A COLORLESS WORLD WAS JUST A DREAM.
I WAS EIGHT YEARS OLD WHEN I WOKE UP TO REALITY.
IT WAS THE MORNING OF JUNE 29, 2009...
THE DAY I SAW THE TRUTH OF COLOR FOR THE VERY FIRST TIME.

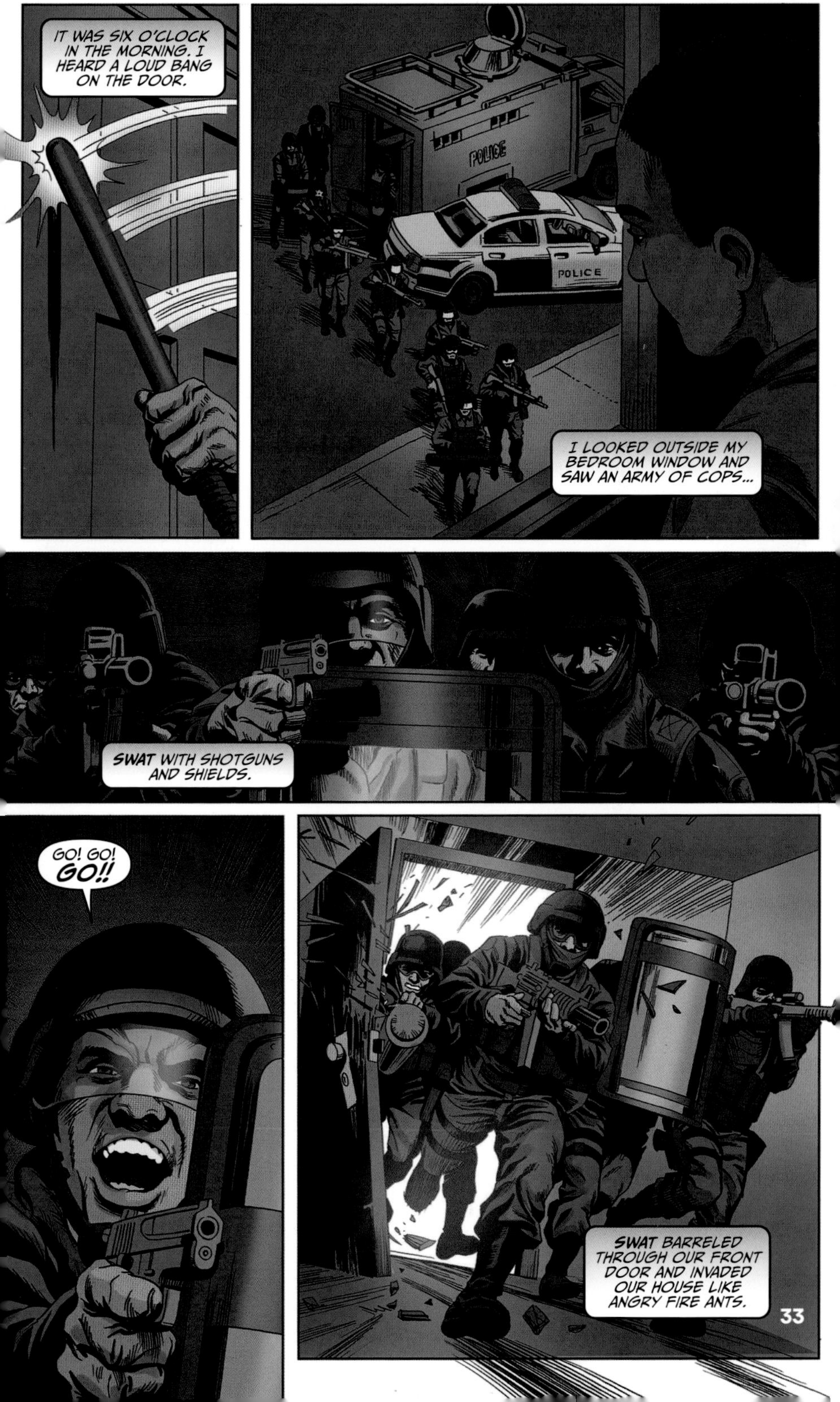
IT WAS SIX O'CLOCK IN THE MORNING. I HEARD A LOUD BANG ON THE DOOR.
POLICE
POLICE
I LOOKED OUTSIDE MY BEDROOM WINDOW AND SAW AN ARMY OF COPS...
SWAT WITH SHOTGUNS AND SHIELDS.
GO! GO! GO!!
SWAT BARRELED THROUGH OUR FRONT DOOR AND INVADED OUR HOUSE LIKE ANGRY FIRE ANTS.

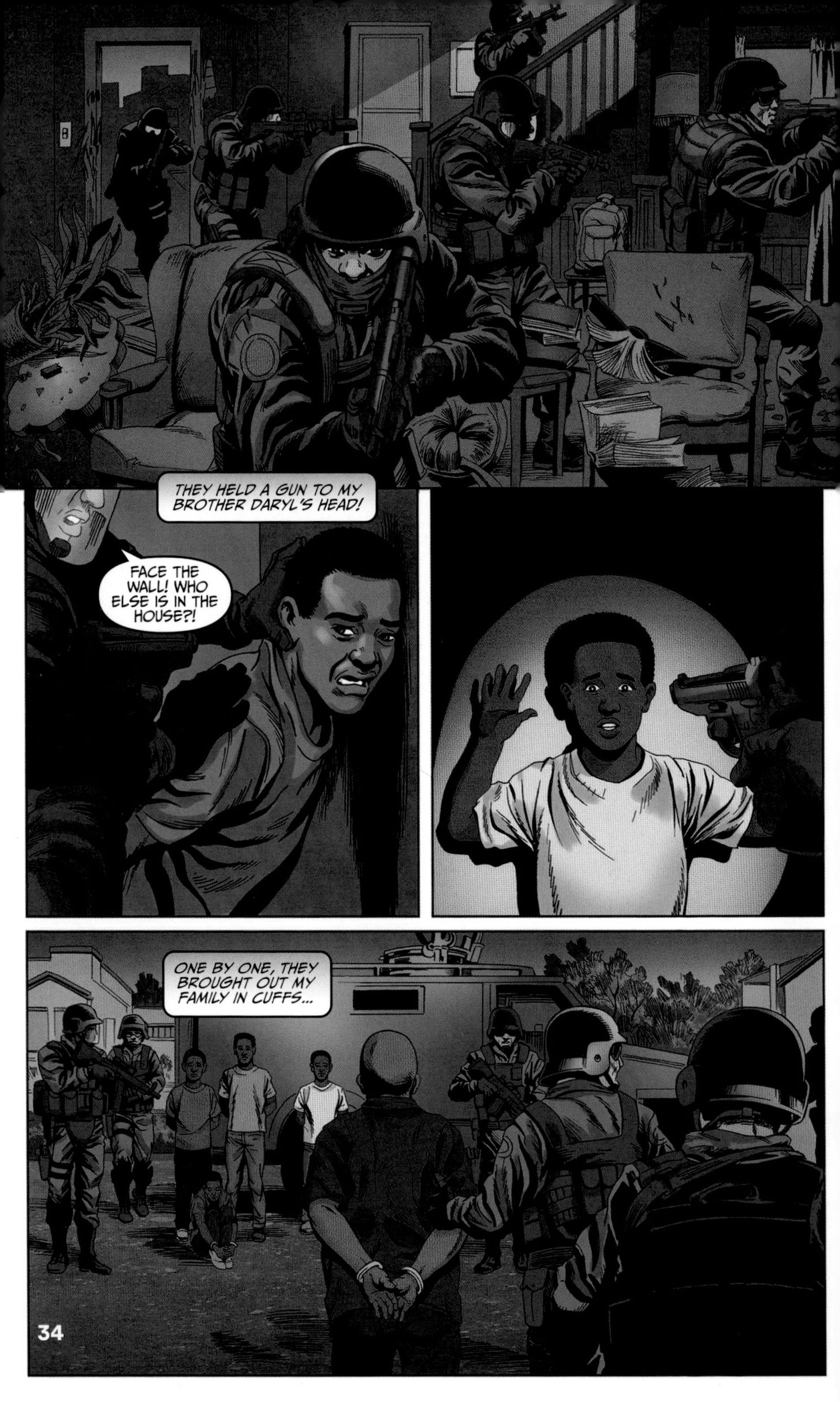
THEY HELD A GUN TO MY BROTHER DARYL'S HEAD!
FACE THE WALL! WHO ELSE IS IN THE HOUSE?!
ONE BY ONE, THEY BROUGHT OUT MY FAMILY IN CUFFS...

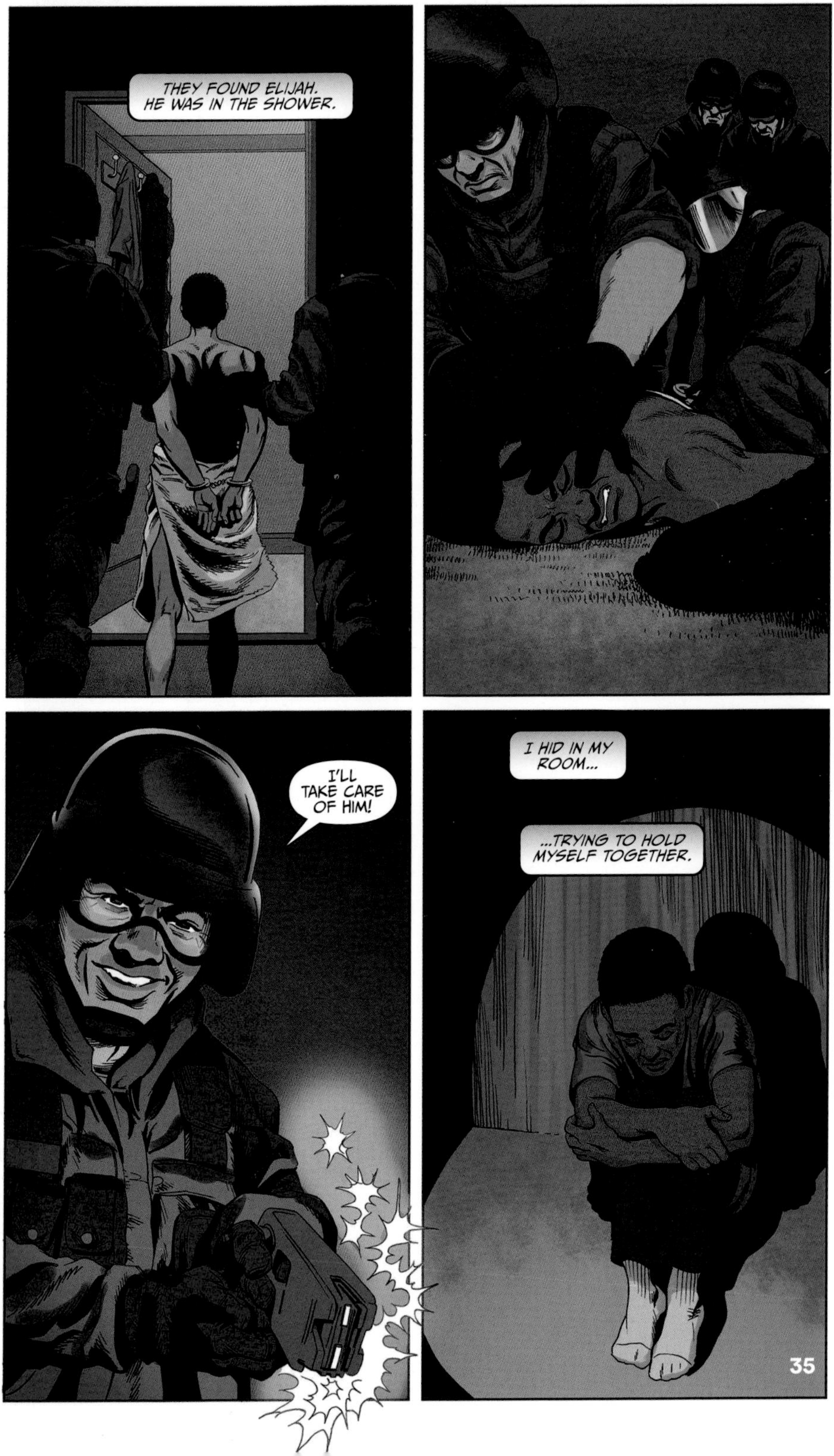
THEY FOUND ELIJAH. HE WAS IN THE SHOWER.
I'LL TAKE CARE OF HIM!
I HID IN MY ROOM...
...TRYING TO HOLD MYSELF TOGETHER.

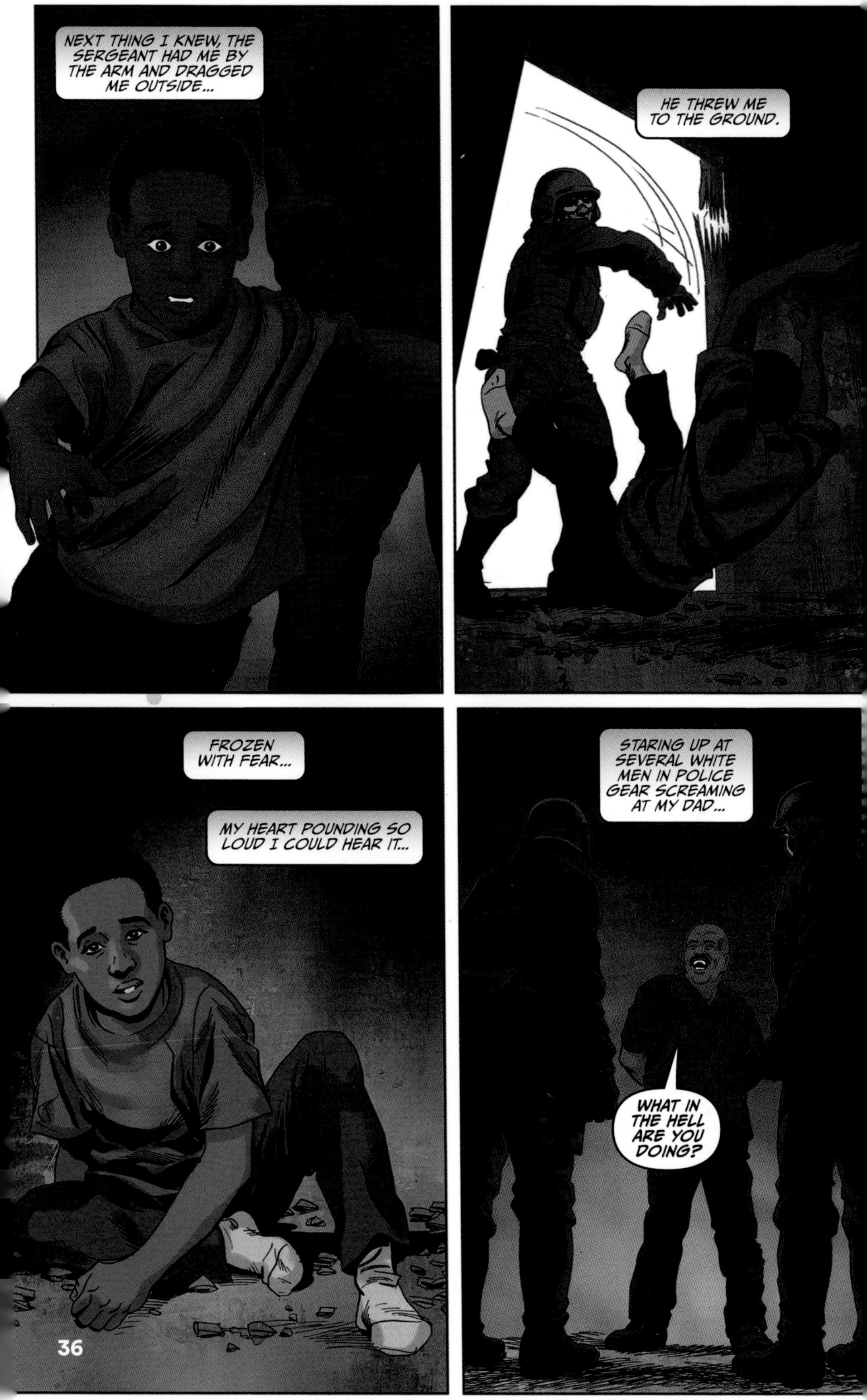

NEXT THING I KNEW, THE SERGEANT HAD ME BY THE ARM AND DRAGGED ME OUTSIDE...
HE THREW ME TO THE GROUND.
FROZEN WITH FEAR...
MY HEART POUNDING SO LOUD I COULD HEAR IT...
STARING UP AT SEVERAL WHITE MEN IN POLICE GEAR SCREAMING AT MY DAD...
WHAT IN THE HELL ARE YOU DOING?

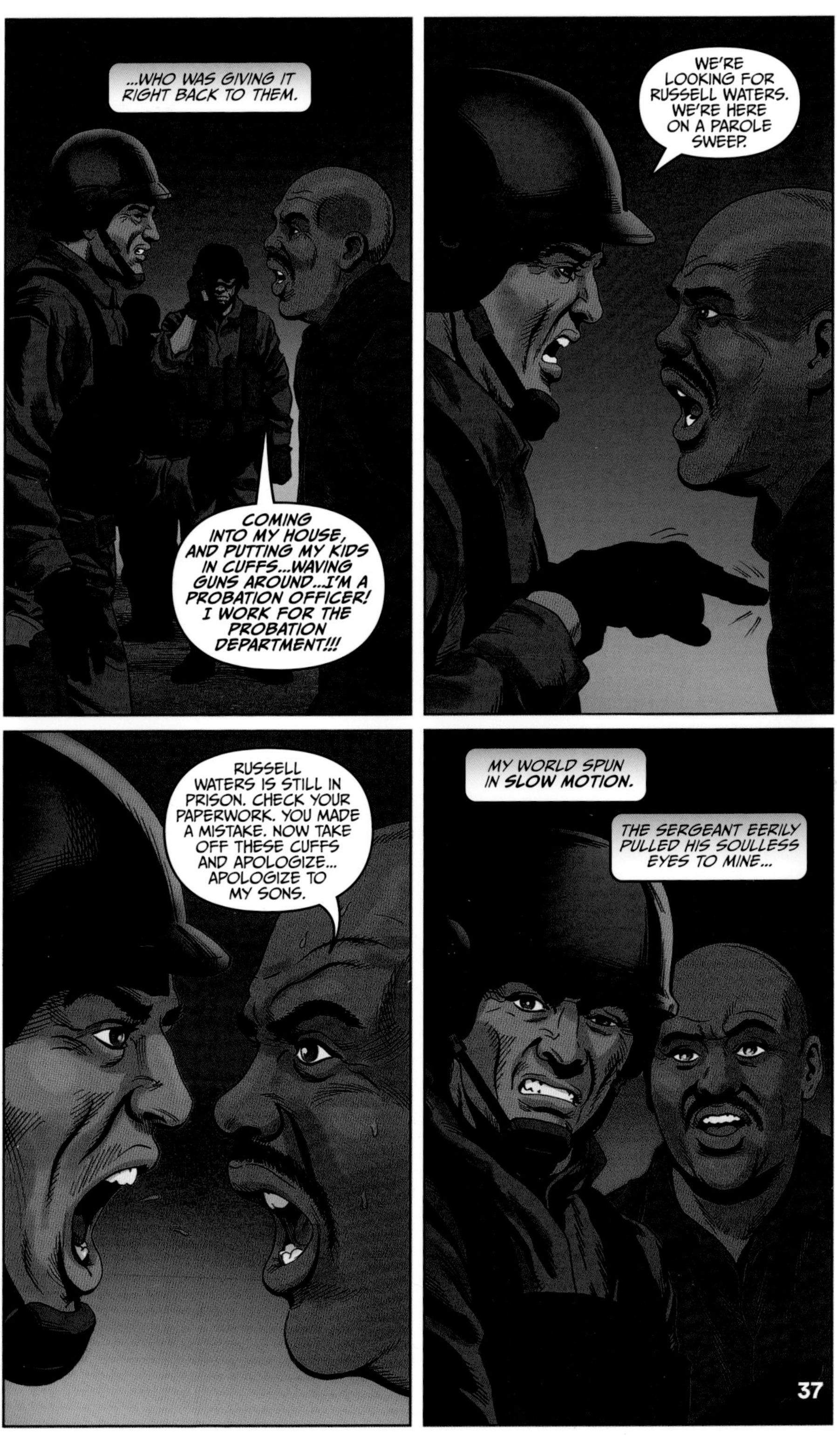
...WHO WAS GIVING IT RIGHT BACK TO THEM.
COMING INTO MY HOUSE, AND PUTTING MY KIDS IN CUFFS...WAVING GUNS AROUND...I'M A PROBATION OFFICER! I WORK FOR THE PROBATION DEPARTMENT!!!
WE'RE LOOKING FOR RUSSELL WATERS. WE'RE HERE ON A PAROLE SWEEP.
RUSSELL WATERS IS STILL IN PRISON. CHECK YOUR PAPERWORK. YOU MADE A MISTAKE. NOW TAKE OFF THESE CUFFS AND APOLOGIZE... APOLOGIZE TO MY SONS.
MY WORLD SPUN IN SLOW MOTION.
THE SERGEANT EERILY PULLED HIS SOULLESS EYES TO MINE...

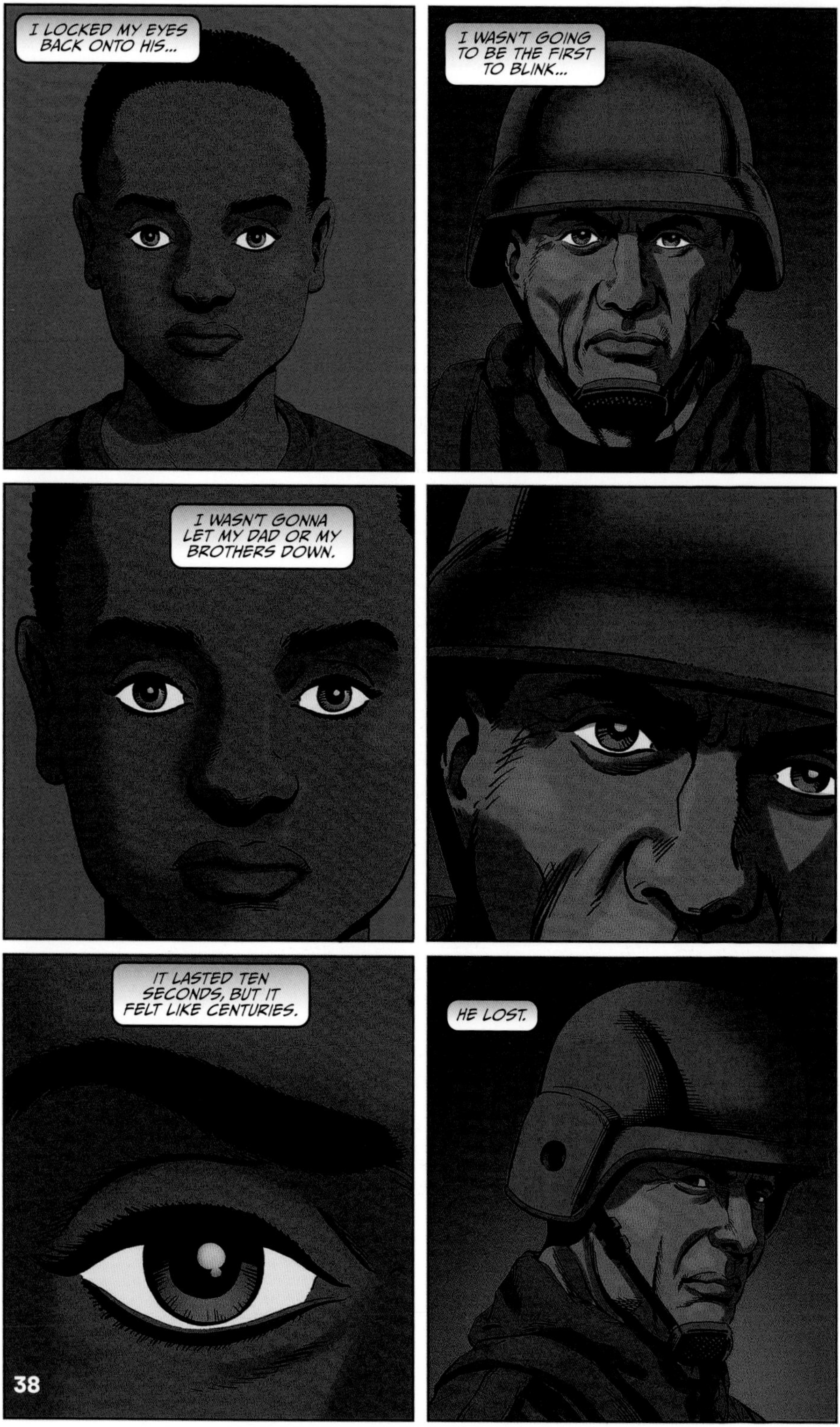
I LOCKED MY EYES BACK ONTO HIS...
I WASN'T GOING TO BE THE FIRST TO BLINK...
I WASN'T GONNA LET MY DAD OR MY BROTHERS DOWN.
IT LASTED TEN SECONDS, BUT IT FELT LIKE CENTURIES.
HE LOST.

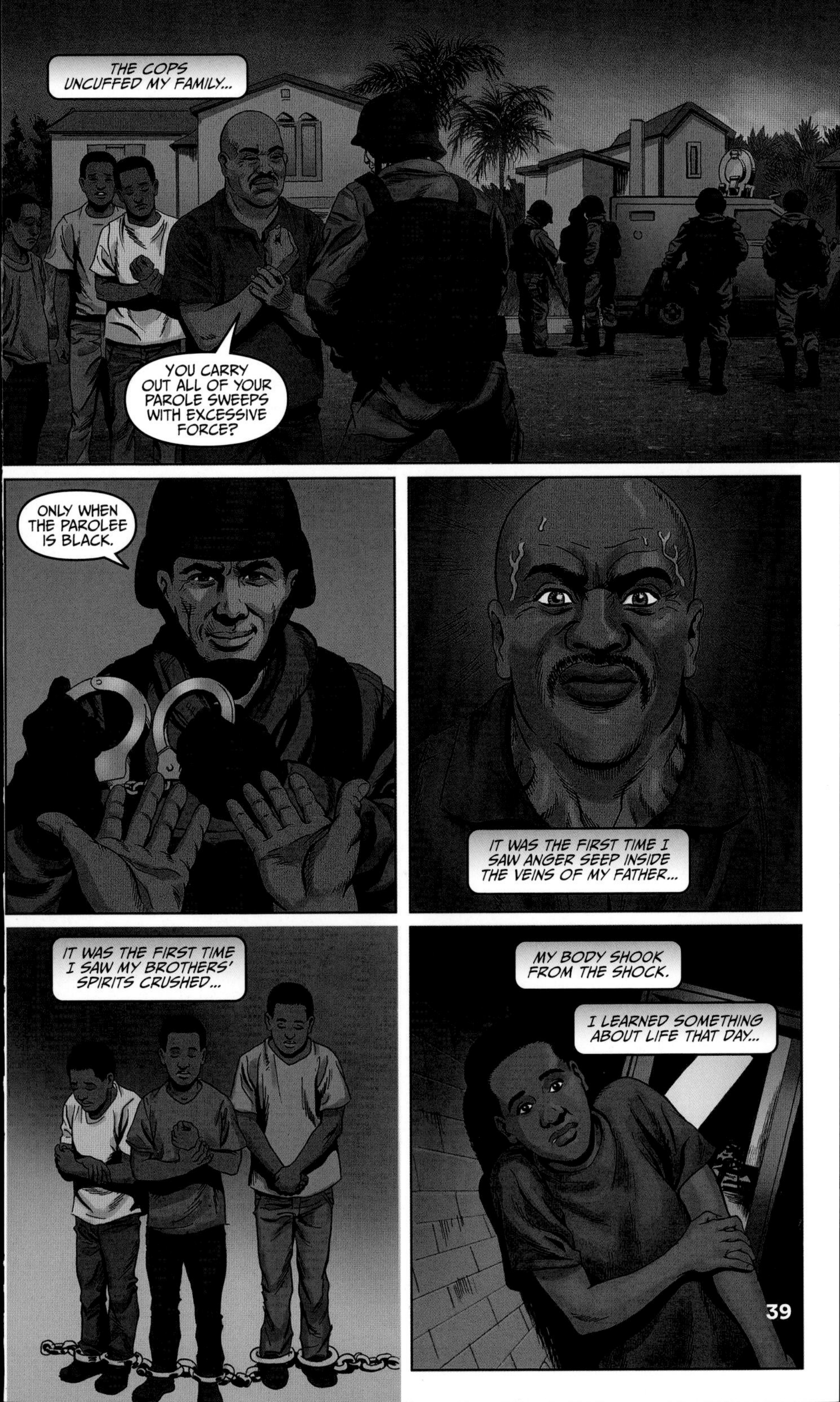
THE COPS UNCUFFED MY FAMILY...
YOU CARRY OUT ALL OF YOUR PAROLE SWEEPS WITH EXCESSIVE FORCE?
ONLY WHEN THE PAROLEE IS BLACK.
IT WAS THE FIRST TIME I SAW ANGER SEEP INSIDE THE VEINS OF MY FATHER...
IT WAS THE FIRST TIME I SAW MY BROTHERS' SPIRITS CRUSHED...
MY BODY SHOOK FROM THE SHOCK.
I LEARNED SOMETHING ABOUT LIFE THAT DAY...

LIFE CAN TURN AGAINST YOU IN THE BLINK OF AN EYE, SO YOU'D BETTER BE READY.

I LEARNED THAT THE WORLD HAD THE CAPACITY TO BE RACIALLY CRUEL.

AND THE VULGAR DISPLAY OF POWER THOSE MEN HAD OVER US...

...IT RESET ME... BACK TO ZERO.

EVERYTHING UNCLE RUSSELL HAD TAUGHT ME, NOW CONFUSED ME.

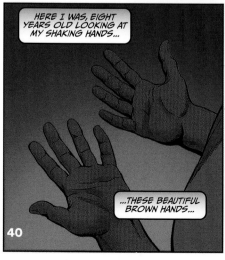

HERE I WAS, EIGHT YEARS OLD LOOKING AT MY SHAKING HANDS...

...THESE BEAUTIFUL BROWN HANDS...

...BALLED UP INTO FISTS.

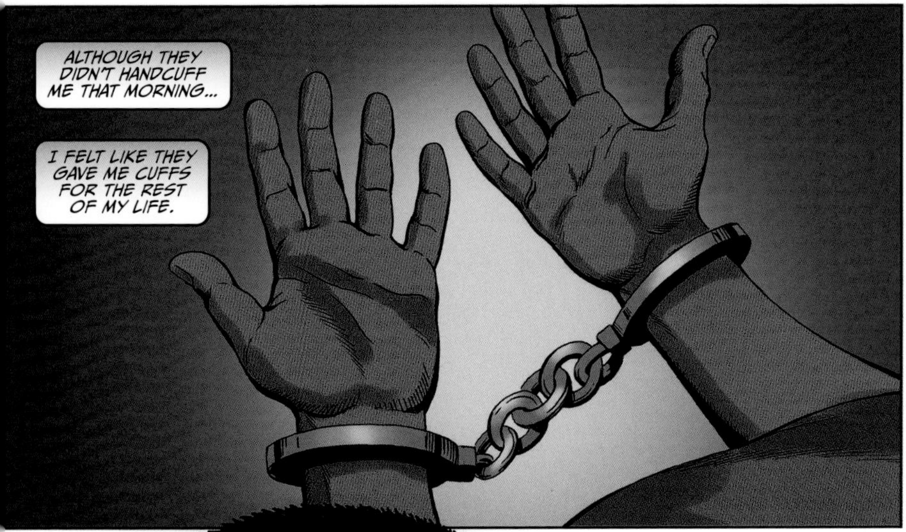
ALTHOUGH THEY DIDN'T HANDCUFF ME THAT MORNING...
I FELT LIKE THEY GAVE ME CUFFS FOR THE REST OF MY LIFE.

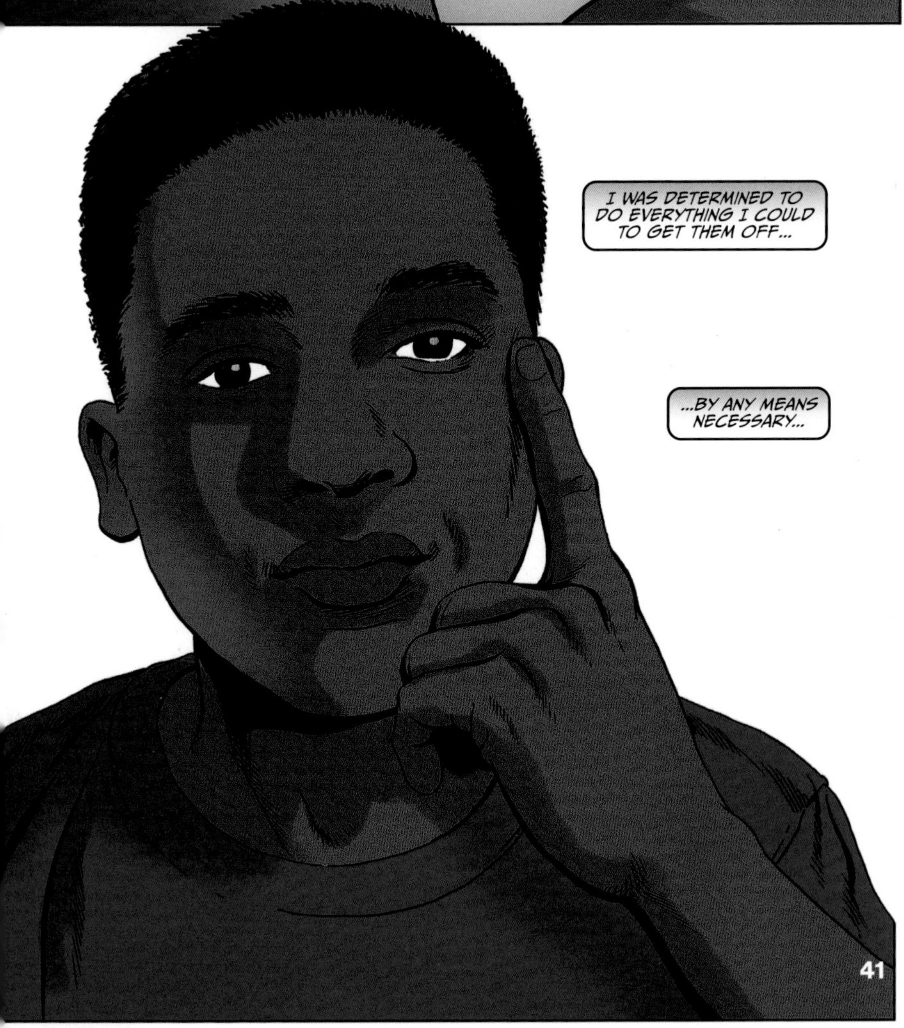
I WAS DETERMINED TO DO EVERYTHING I COULD TO GET THEM OFF...
...BY ANY MEANS NECESSARY...

LAST THING MY MOM WANTED WAS A SON GROWING UP IN THE WORLD ANGRY AND BITTER.

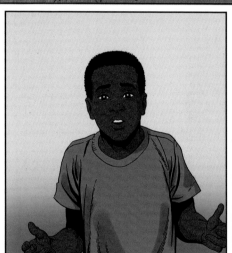

MOM WASN'T HAVING IT...

42

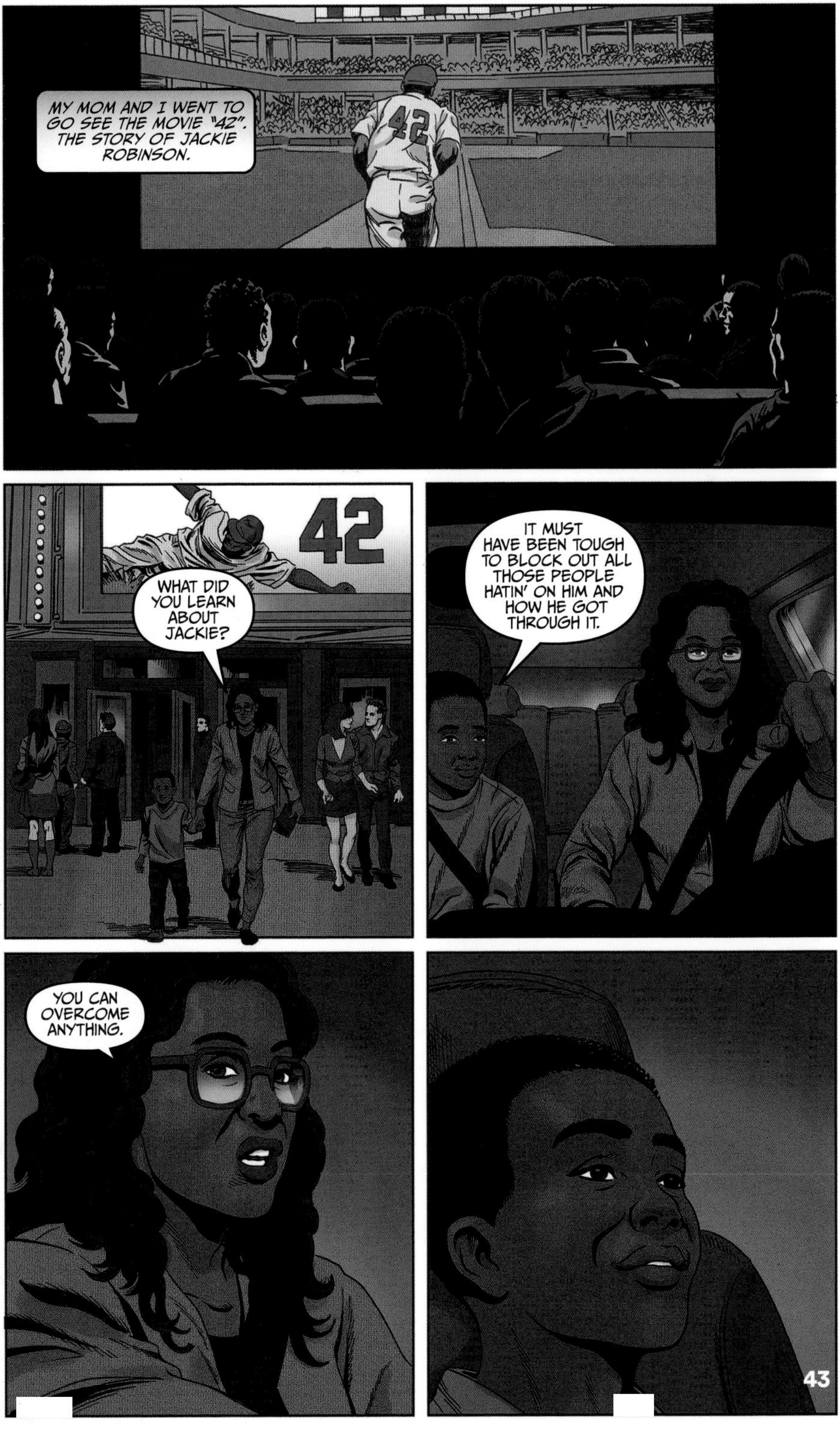
MY MOM AND I WENT TO GO SEE THE MOVIE "42". THE STORY OF JACKIE ROBINSON.
42
WHAT DID YOU LEARN ABOUT JACKIE?
IT MUST HAVE BEEN TOUGH TO BLOCK OUT ALL THOSE PEOPLE HATIN' ON HIM AND HOW HE GOT THROUGH IT.
YOU CAN OVERCOME ANYTHING.

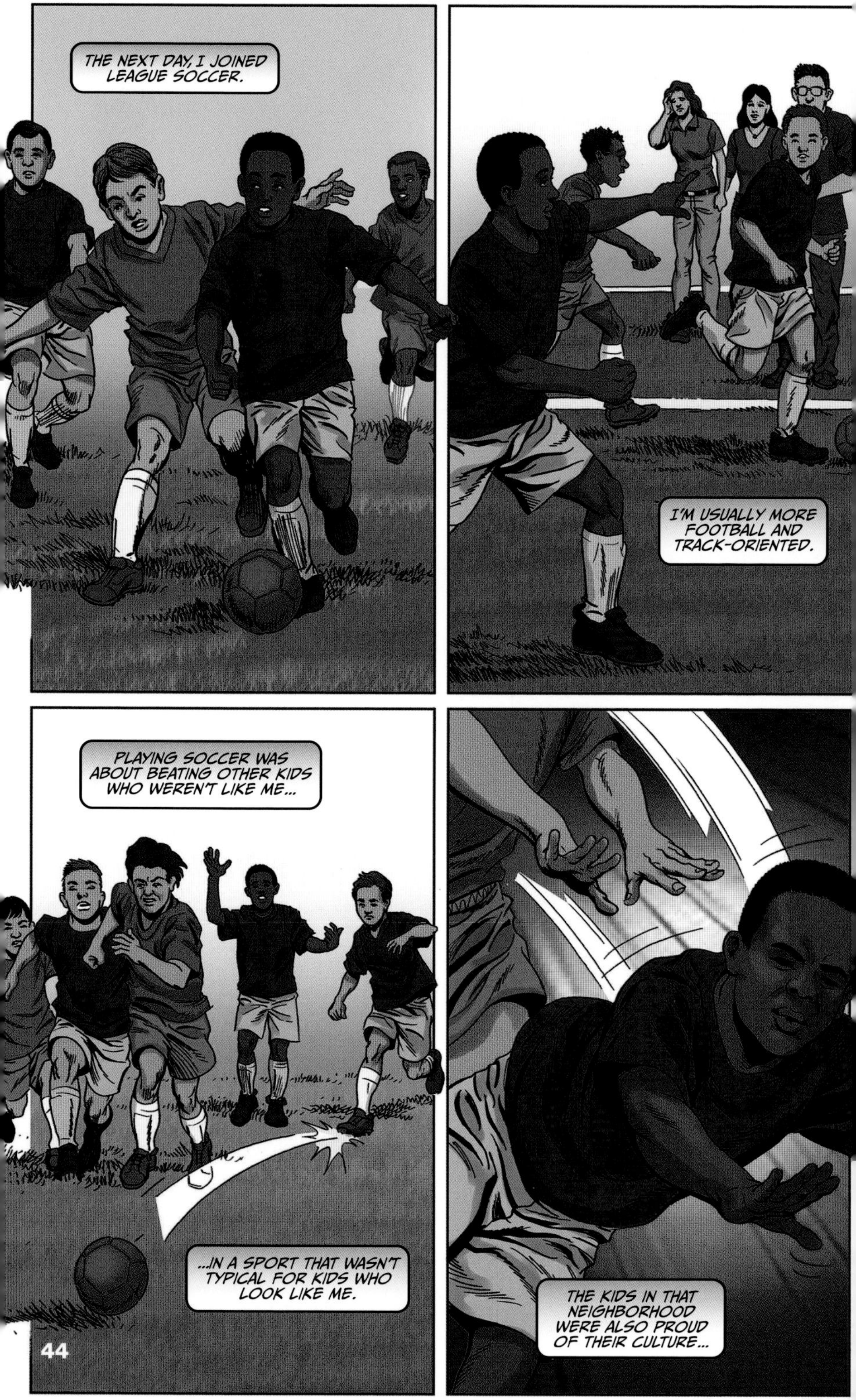
THE NEXT DAY, I JOINED LEAGUE SOCCER.
I'M USUALLY MORE FOOTBALL AND TRACK-ORIENTED.
PLAYING SOCCER WAS ABOUT BEATING OTHER KIDS WHO WEREN'T LIKE ME...
...IN A SPORT THAT WASN'T TYPICAL FOR KIDS WHO LOOK LIKE ME.
THE KIDS IN THAT NEIGHBORHOOD WERE ALSO PROUD OF THEIR CULTURE...

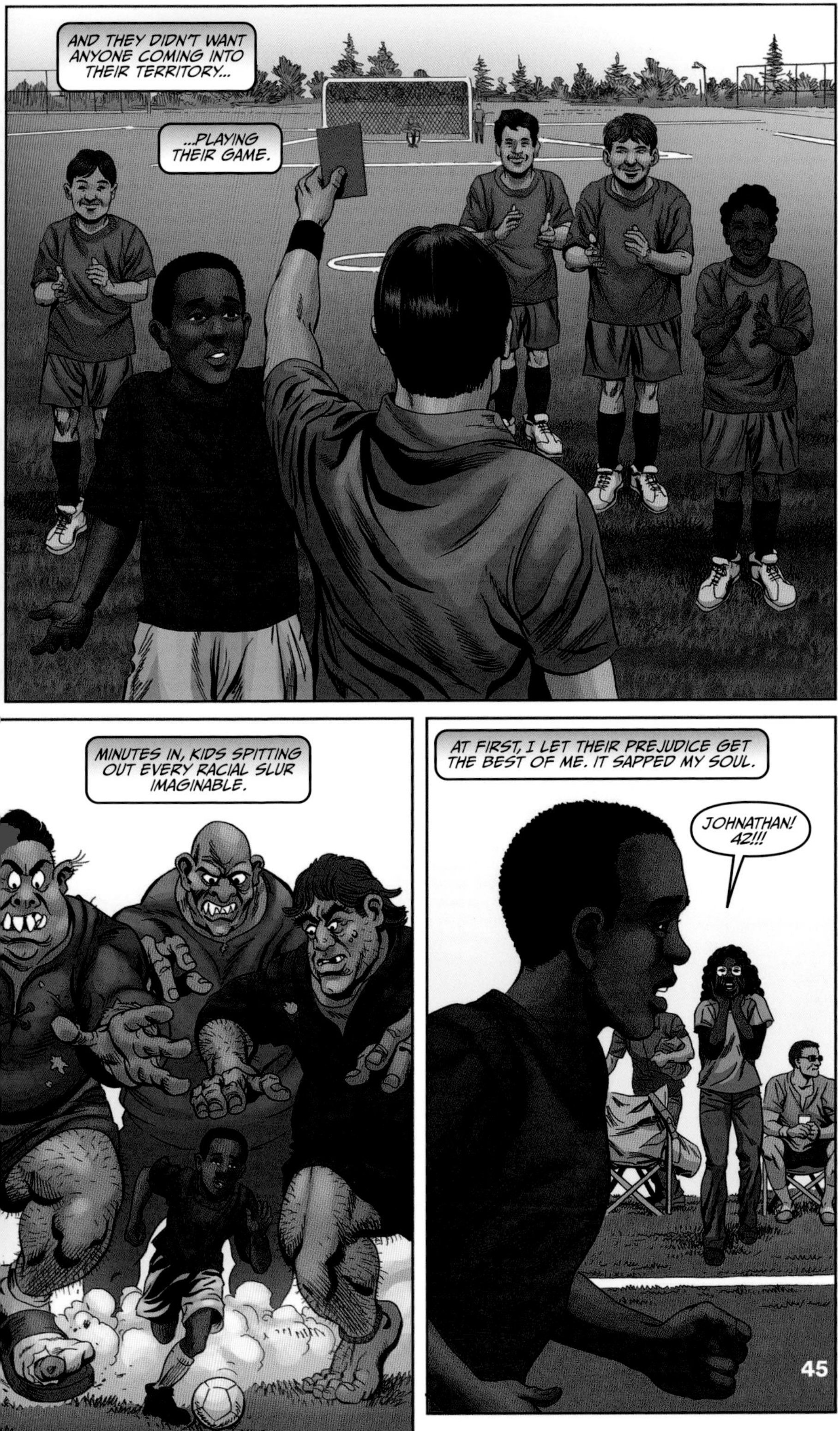
AND THEY DIDN'T WANT ANYONE COMING INTO THEIR TERRITORY...
...PLAYING THEIR GAME.
MINUTES IN, KIDS SPITTING OUT EVERY RACIAL SLUR IMAGINABLE.
AT FIRST, I LET THEIR PREJUDICE GET THE BEST OF ME. IT SAPPED MY SOUL.
JOHNATHAN! 42!!!

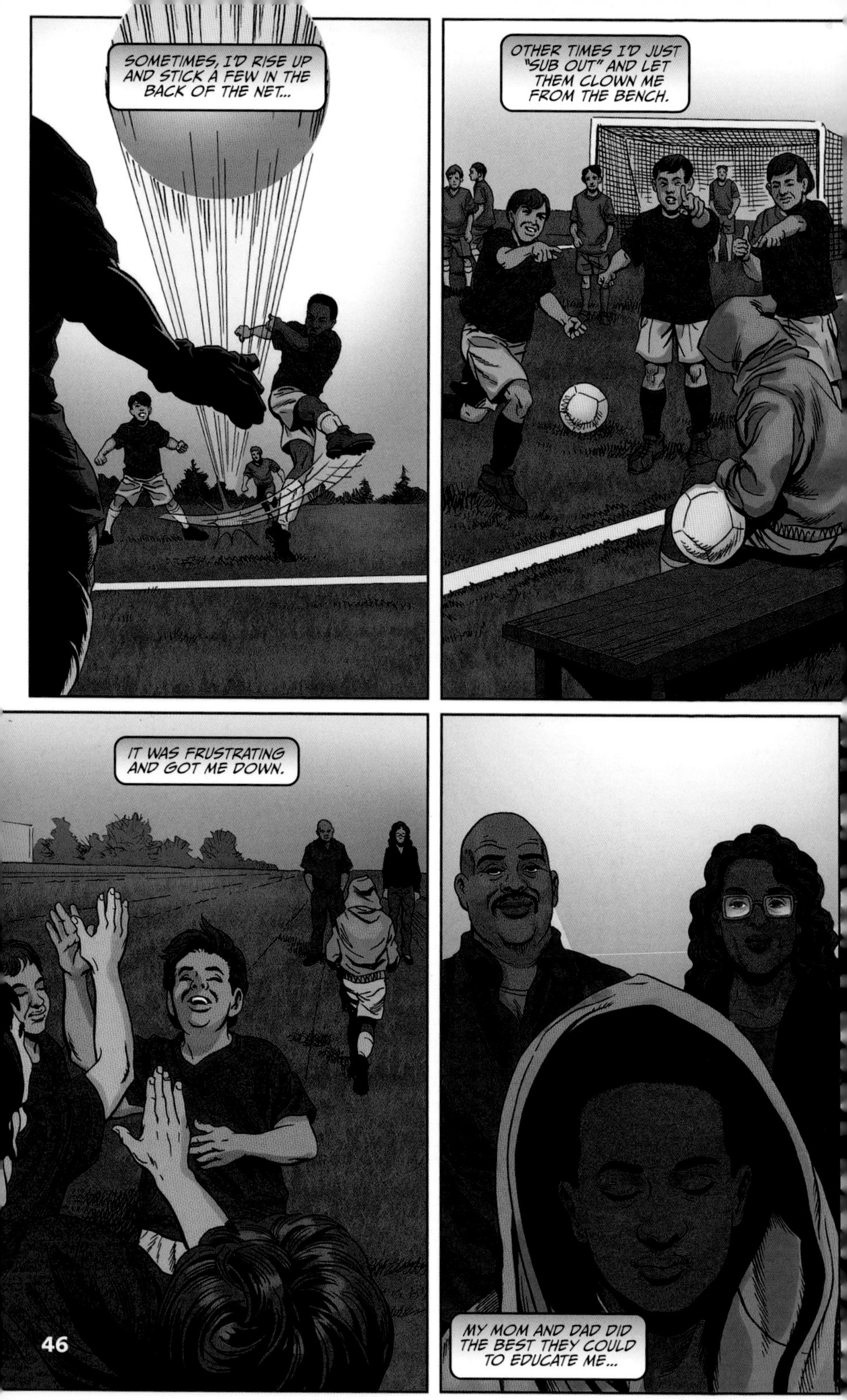
SOMETIMES, I'D RISE UP AND STICK A FEW IN THE BACK OF THE NET...
OTHER TIMES I'D JUST "SUB OUT" AND LET THEM CLOWN ME FROM THE BENCH.
IT WAS FRUSTRATING AND GOT ME DOWN.
MY MOM AND DAD DID THE BEST THEY COULD TO EDUCATE ME...

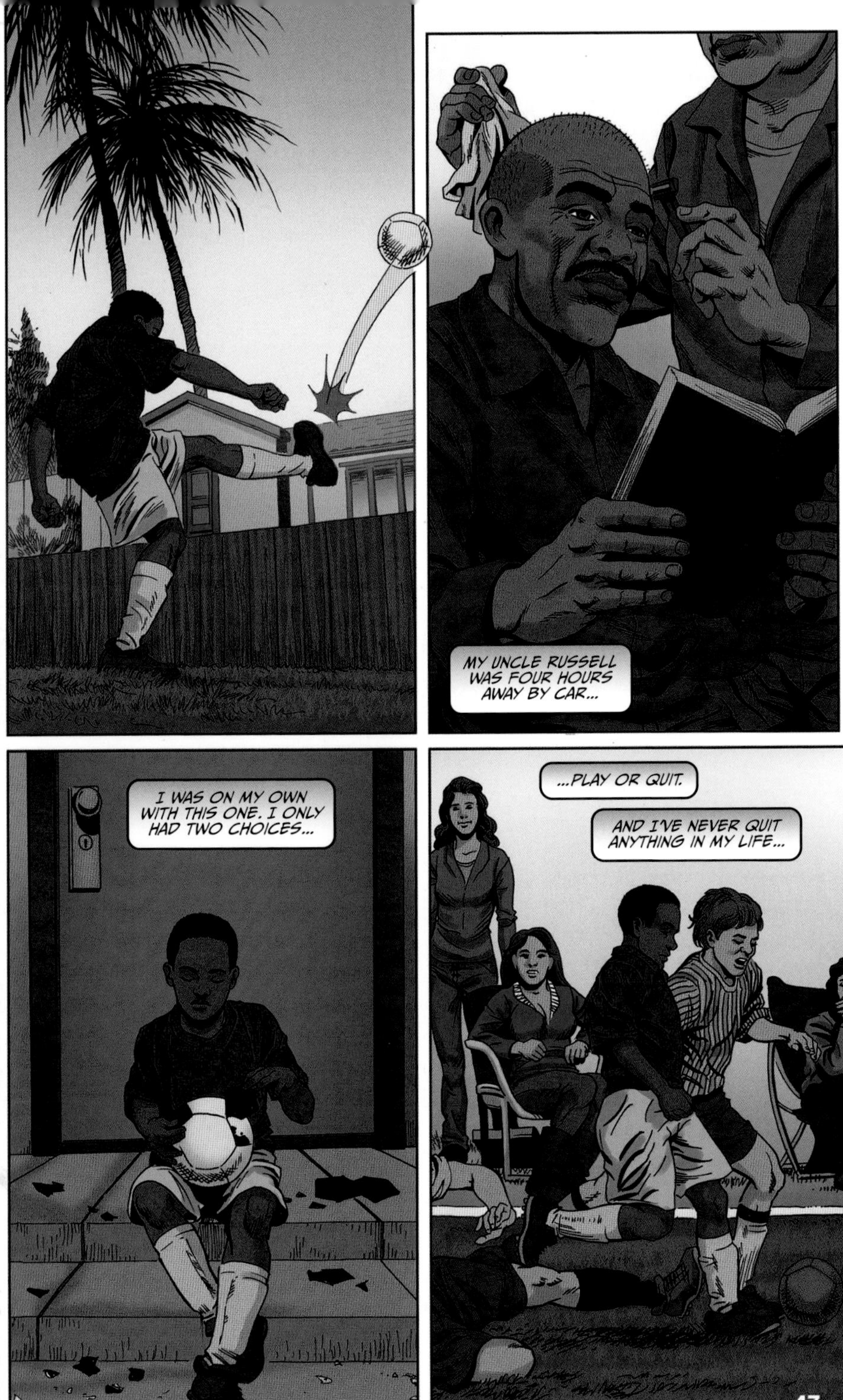
MY UNCLE RUSSELL WAS FOUR HOURS AWAY BY CAR...
I WAS ON MY OWN WITH THIS ONE. I ONLY HAD TWO CHOICES...
...PLAY OR QUIT.
AND I'VE NEVER QUIT ANYTHING IN MY LIFE...

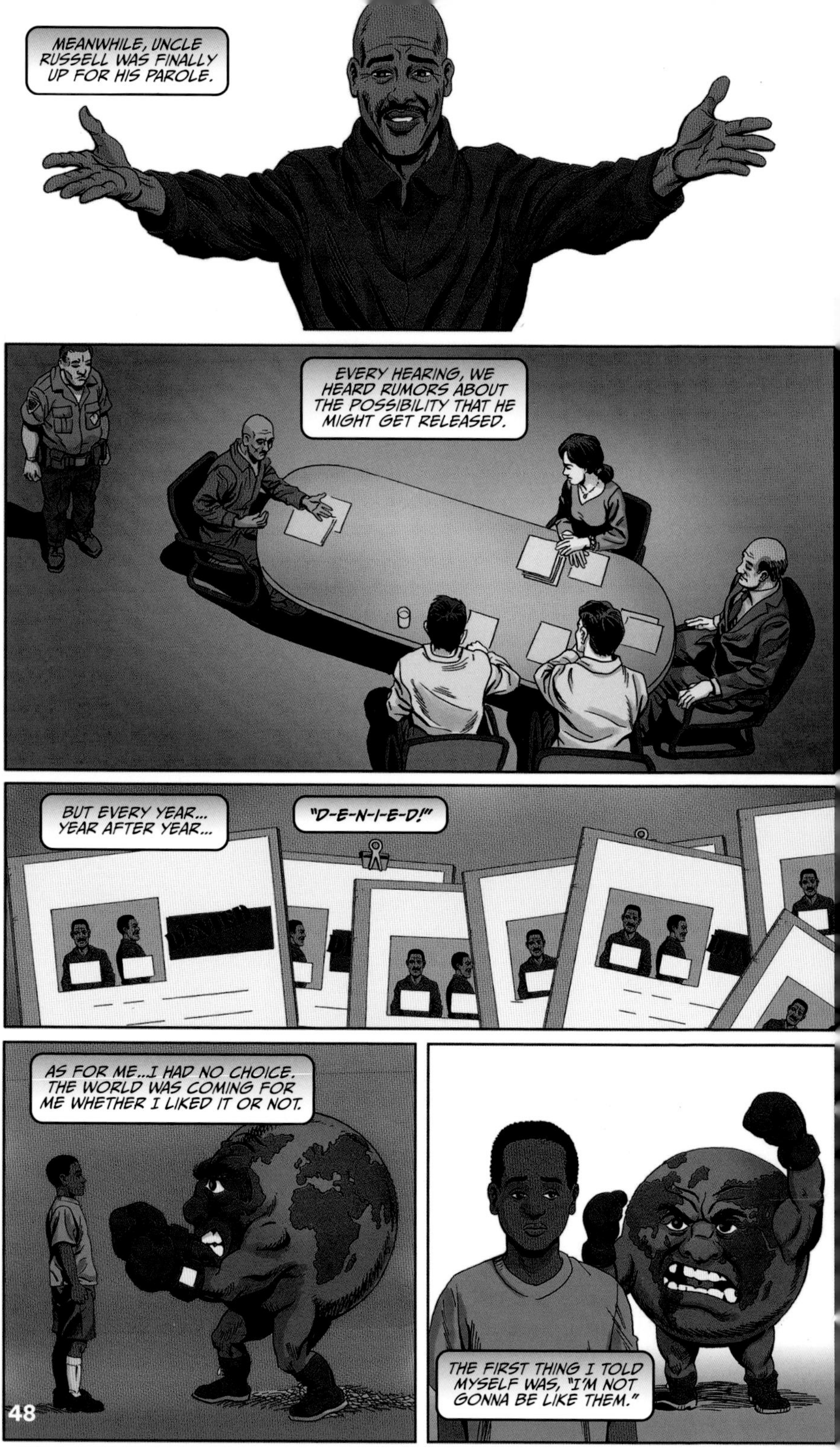
MEANWHILE, UNCLE RUSSELL WAS FINALLY UP FOR HIS PAROLE.
EVERY HEARING, WE HEARD RUMORS ABOUT THE POSSIBILITY THAT HE MIGHT GET RELEASED.
BUT EVERY YEAR... YEAR AFTER YEAR...
"D-E-N-I-E-D!"
AS FOR ME...I HAD NO CHOICE. THE WORLD WAS COMING FOR ME WHETHER I LIKED IT OR NOT.
THE FIRST THING I TOLD MYSELF WAS, "I'M NOT GONNA BE LIKE THEM."

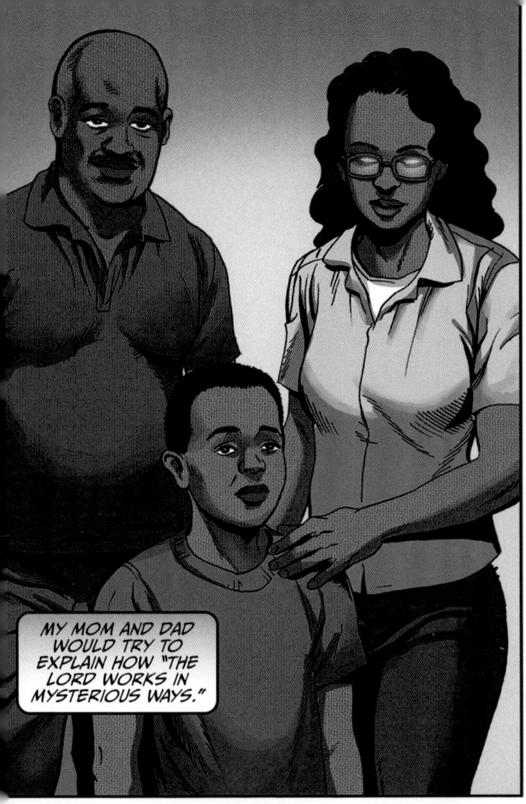
MY MOM AND DAD WOULD TRY TO EXPLAIN HOW "THE LORD WORKS IN MYSTERIOUS WAYS."

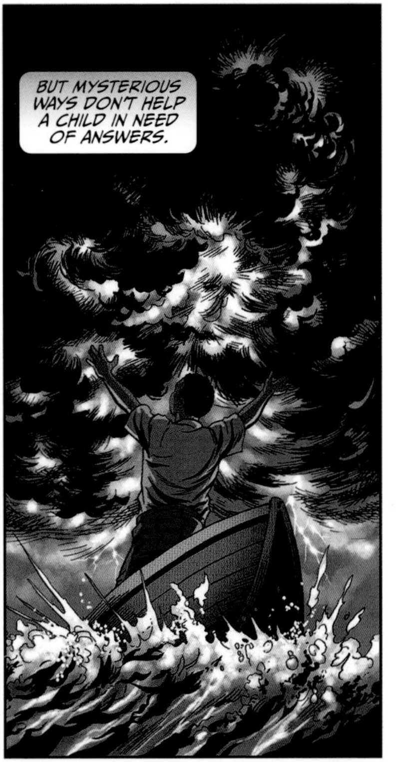
BUT MYSTERIOUS WAYS DON'T HELP A CHILD IN NEED OF ANSWERS.

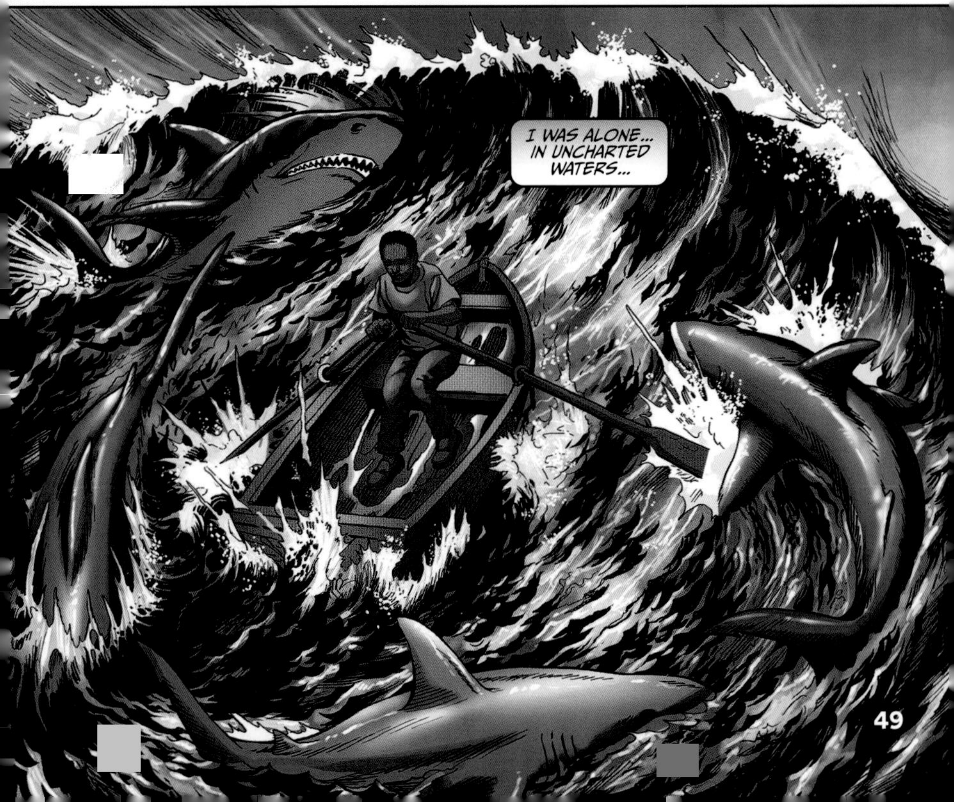
I WAS ALONE... IN UNCHARTED WATERS...

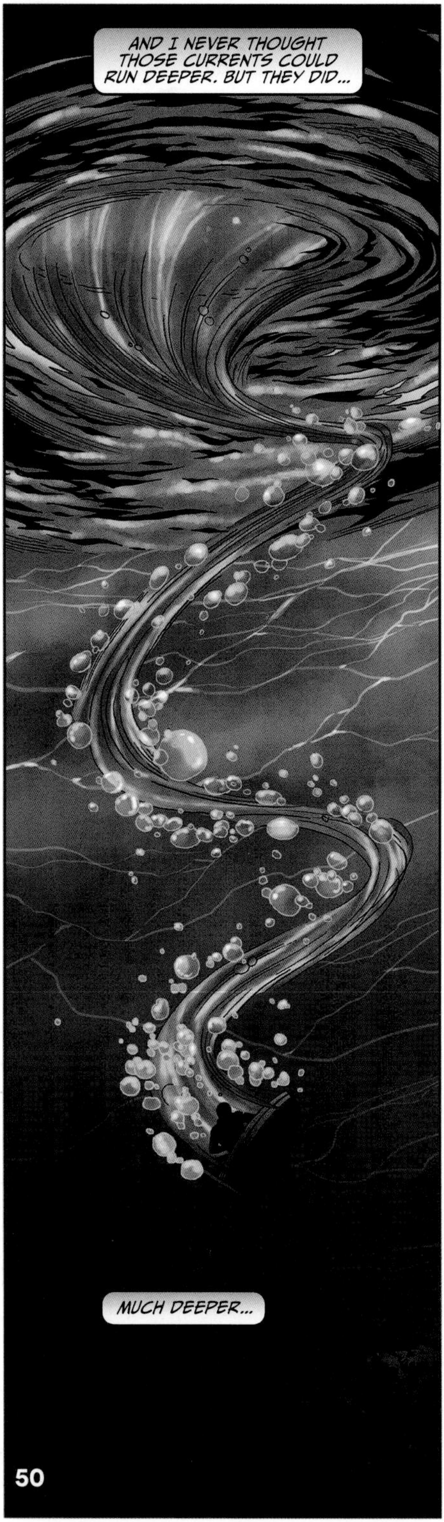
AND I NEVER THOUGHT THOSE CURRENTS COULD RUN DEEPER. BUT THEY DID...
MUCH DEEPER...

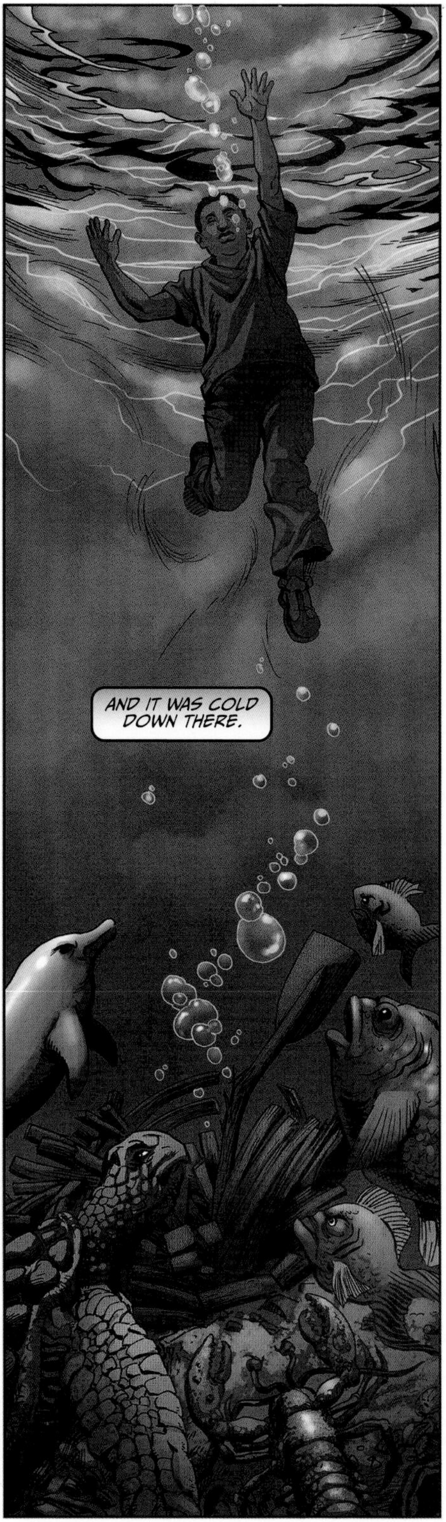
AND IT WAS COLD DOWN THERE.

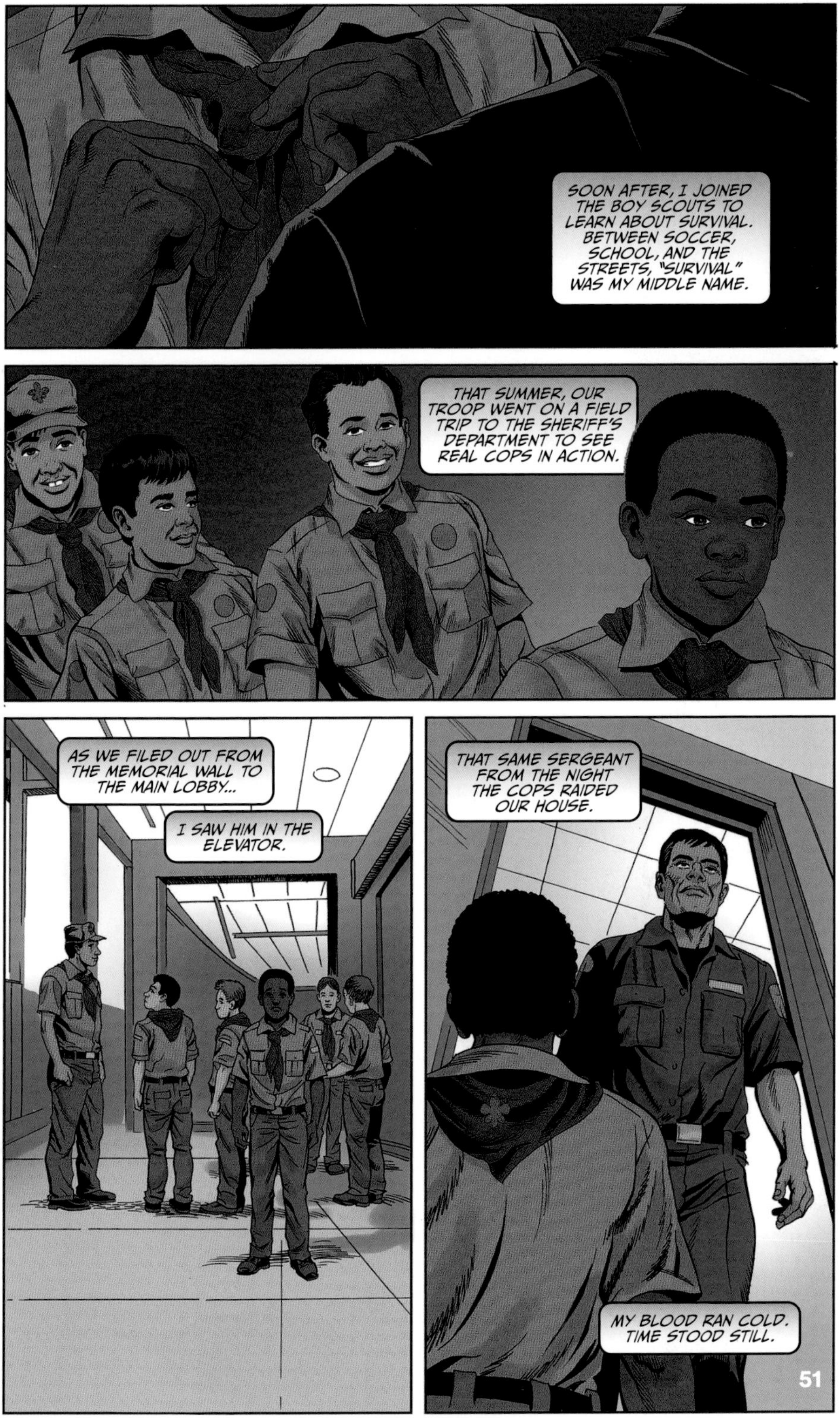
SOON AFTER, I JOINED THE BOY SCOUTS TO LEARN ABOUT SURVIVAL. BETWEEN SOCCER, SCHOOL, AND THE STREETS, "SURVIVAL" WAS MY MIDDLE NAME.
THAT SUMMER, OUR TROOP WENT ON A FIELD TRIP TO THE SHERIFF'S DEPARTMENT TO SEE REAL COPS IN ACTION.
AS WE FILED OUT FROM THE MEMORIAL WALL TO THE MAIN LOBBY...
I SAW HIM IN THE ELEVATOR.
THAT SAME SERGEANT FROM THE NIGHT THE COPS RAIDED OUR HOUSE.
MY BLOOD RAN COLD. TIME STOOD STILL.

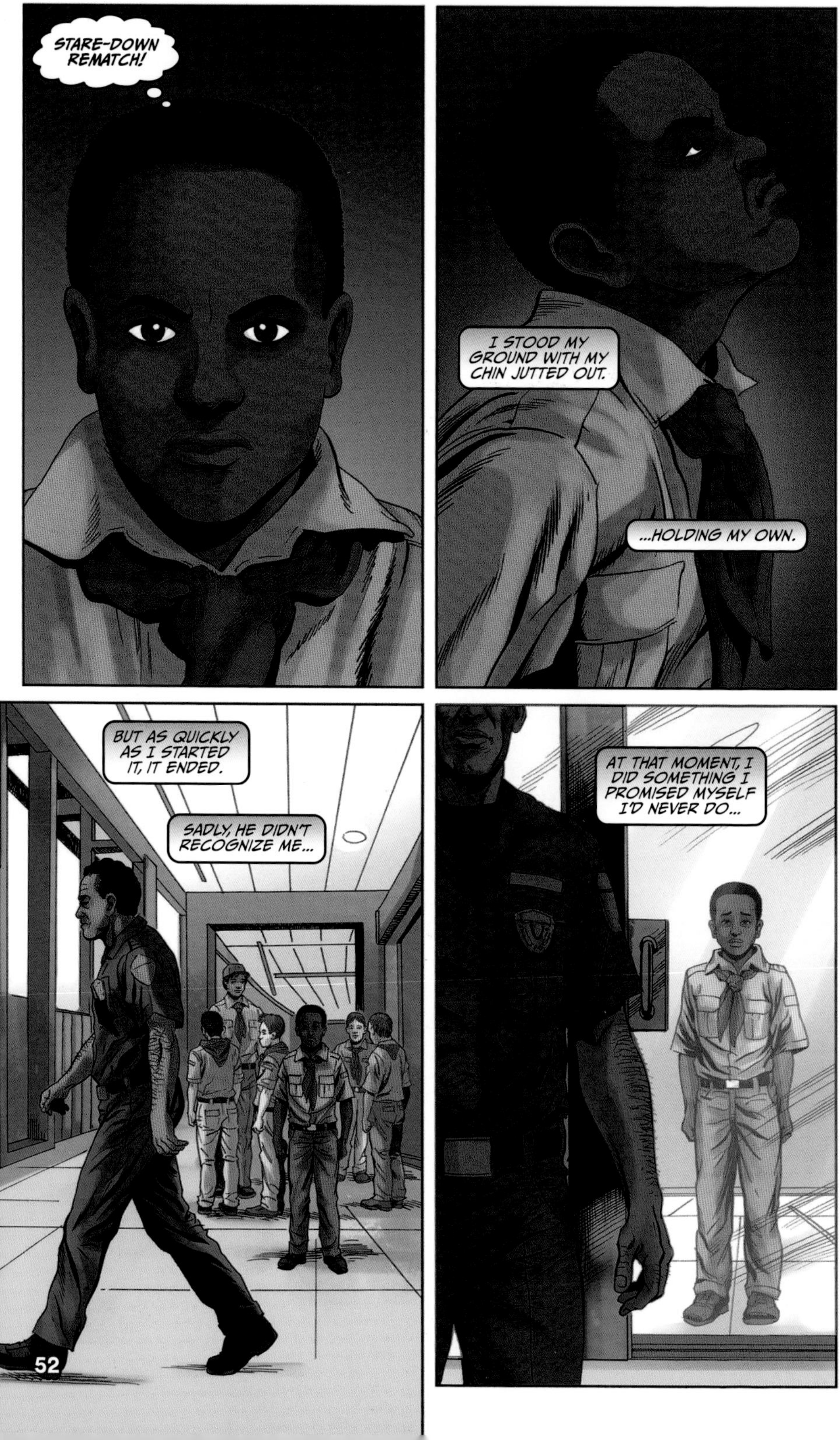
STARE-DOWN REMATCH!
I STOOD MY GROUND WITH MY CHIN JUTTED OUT.
...HOLDING MY OWN.
BUT AS QUICKLY AS I STARTED IT, IT ENDED.
SADLY, HE DIDN'T RECOGNIZE ME...
AT THAT MOMENT, I DID SOMETHING I PROMISED MYSELF I'D NEVER DO...

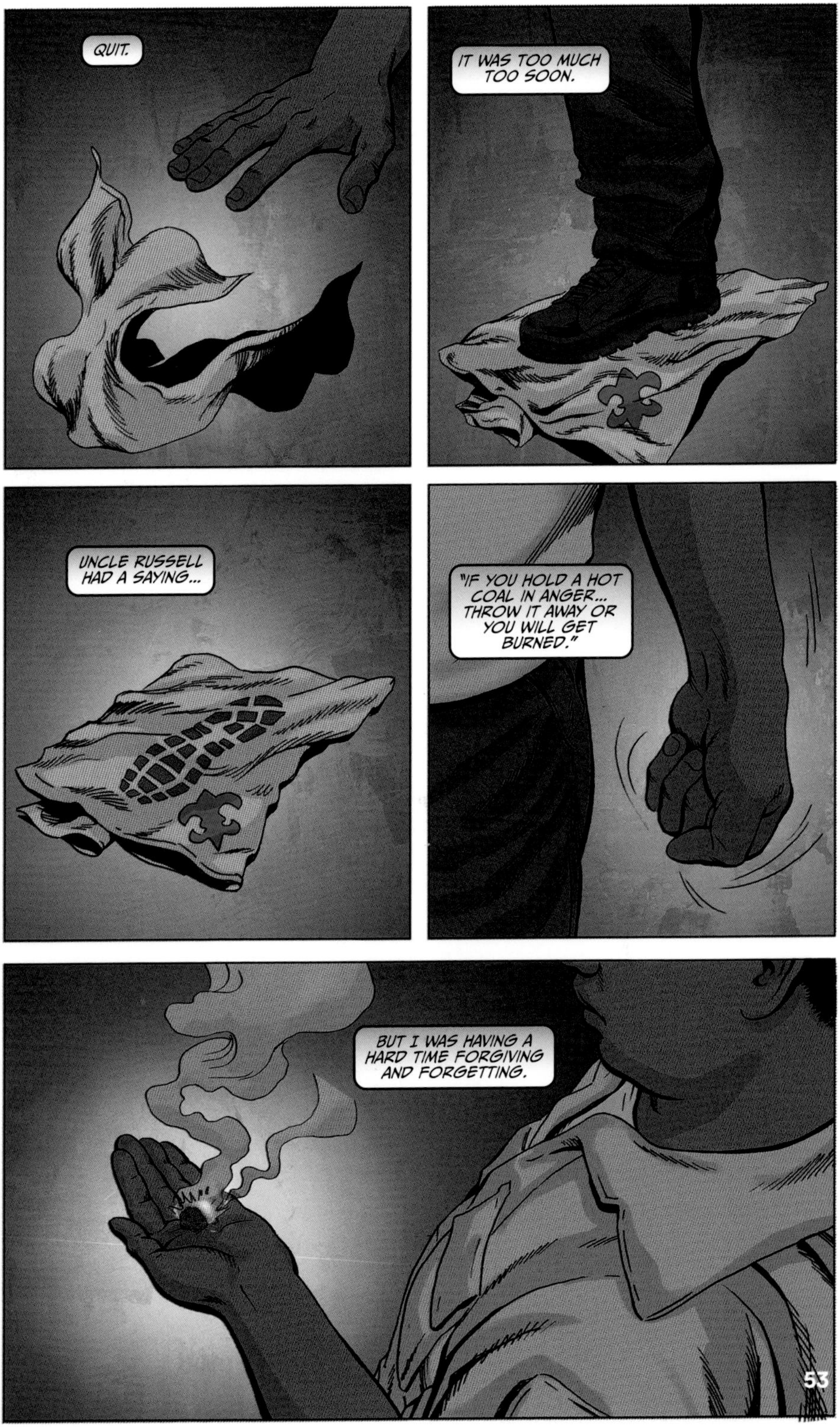
QUIT.
IT WAS TOO MUCH TOO SOON.
UNCLE RUSSELL HAD A SAYING...
"IF YOU HOLD A HOT COAL IN ANGER... THROW IT AWAY OR YOU WILL GET BURNED."
BUT I WAS HAVING A HARD TIME FORGIVING AND FORGETTING.

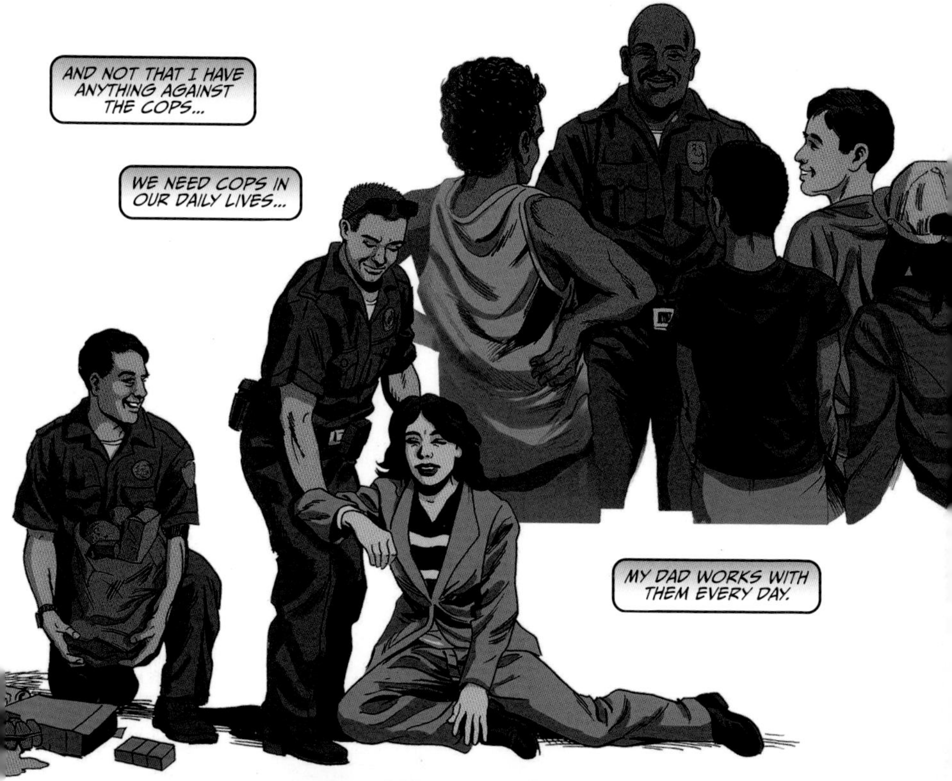
AND NOT THAT I HAVE ANYTHING AGAINST THE COPS...
WE NEED COPS IN OUR DAILY LIVES...
MY DAD WORKS WITH THEM EVERY DAY.

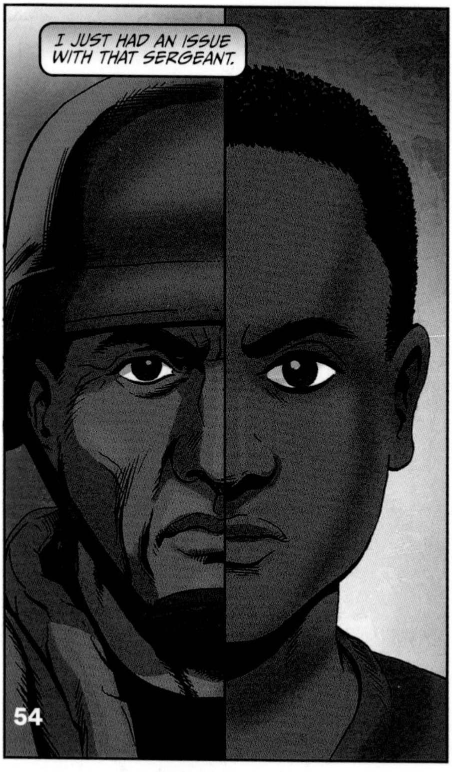
I JUST HAD AN ISSUE WITH THAT SERGEANT.

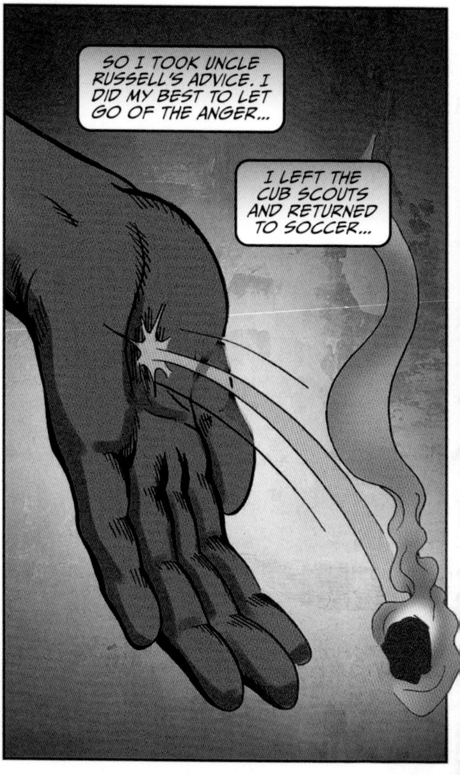
SO I TOOK UNCLE RUSSELL'S ADVICE. I DID MY BEST TO LET GO OF THE ANGER...
I LEFT THE CUB SCOUTS AND RETURNED TO SOCCER...

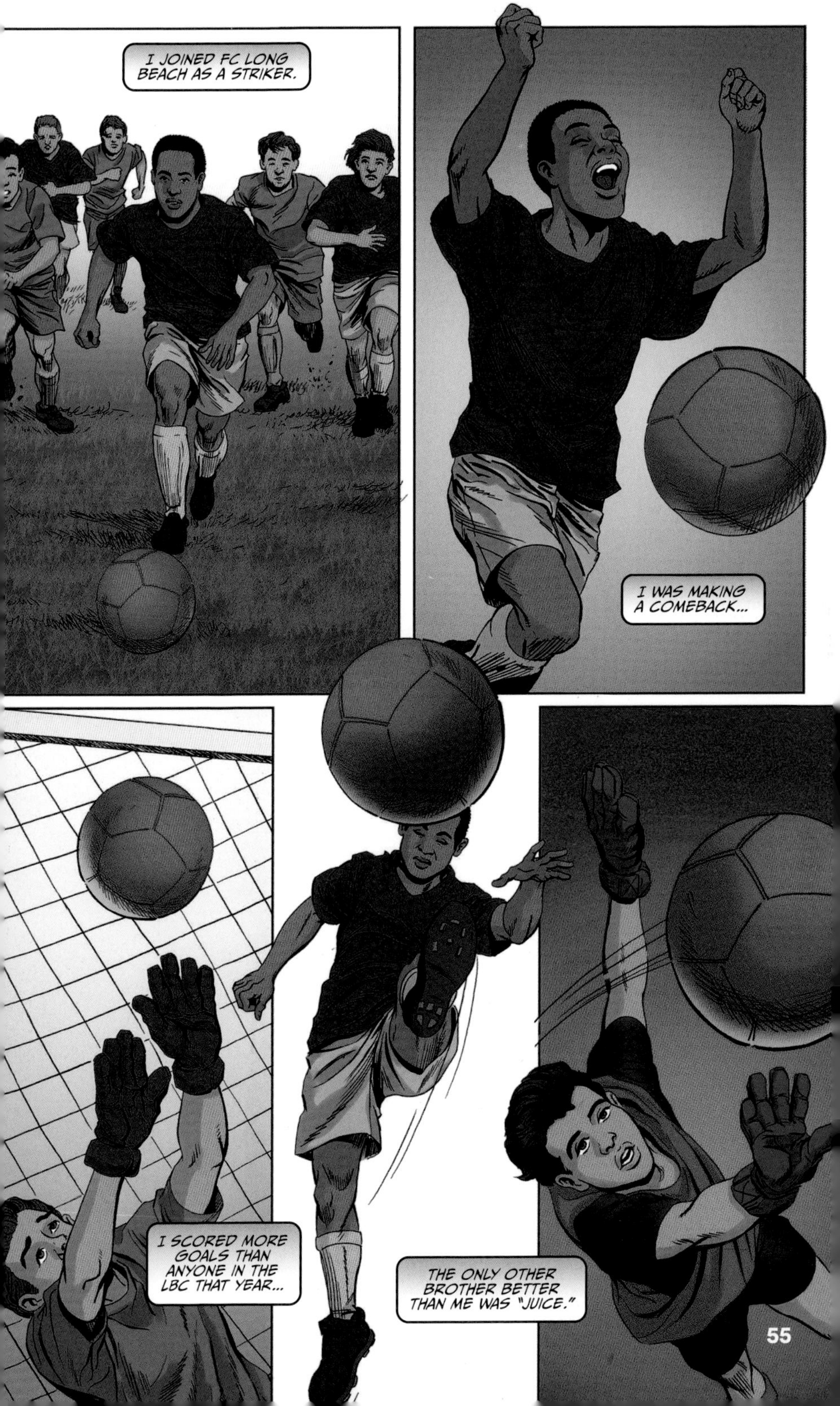
I JOINED FC LONG BEACH AS A STRIKER.
I WAS MAKING A COMEBACK...
I SCORED MORE GOALS THAN ANYONE IN THE LBC THAT YEAR...
THE ONLY OTHER BROTHER BETTER THAN ME WAS "JUICE."

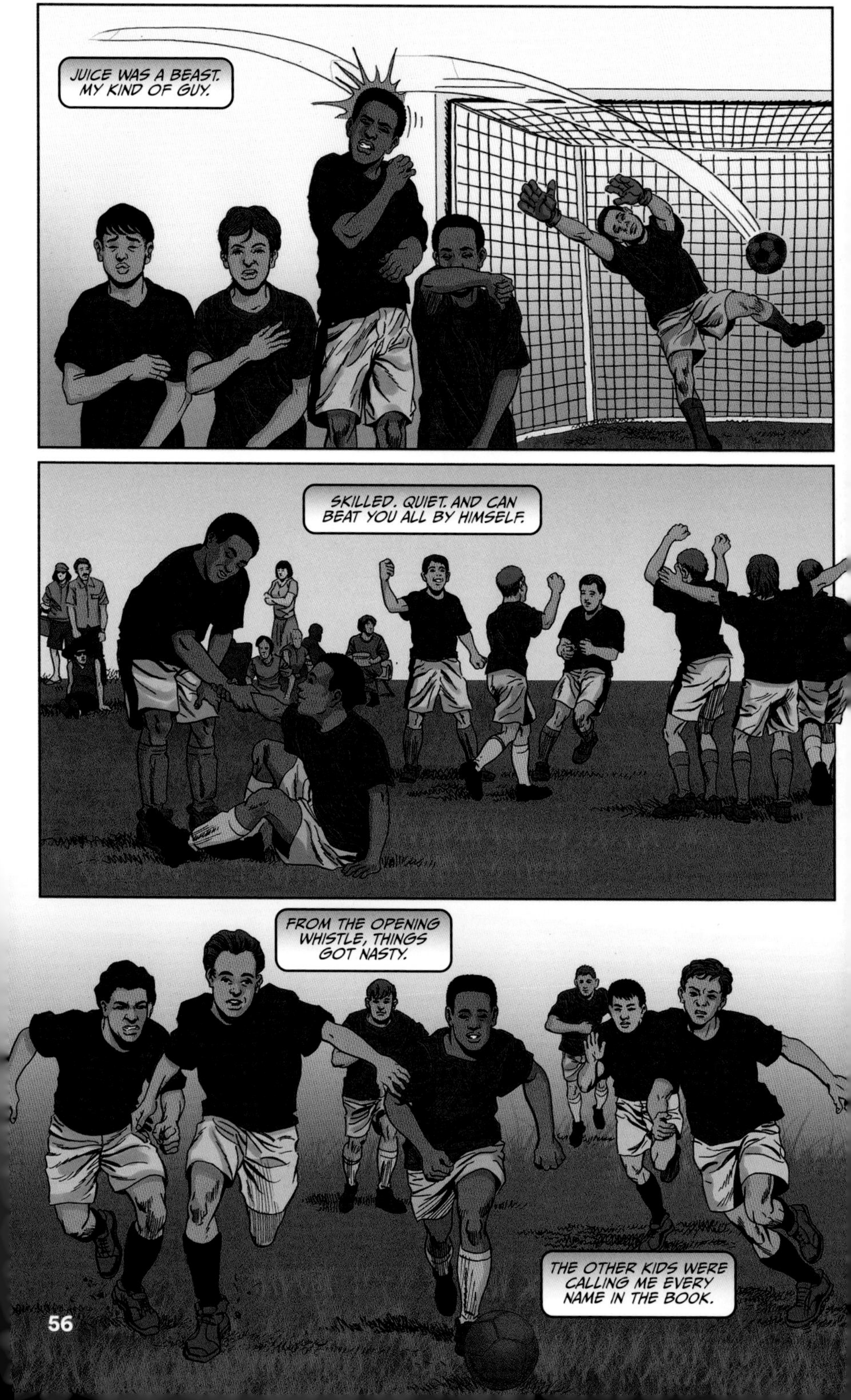
JUICE WAS A BEAST. MY KIND OF GUY.
SKILLED. QUIET. AND CAN BEAT YOU ALL BY HIMSELF.
FROM THE OPENING WHISTLE, THINGS GOT NASTY.
THE OTHER KIDS WERE CALLING ME EVERY NAME IN THE BOOK.

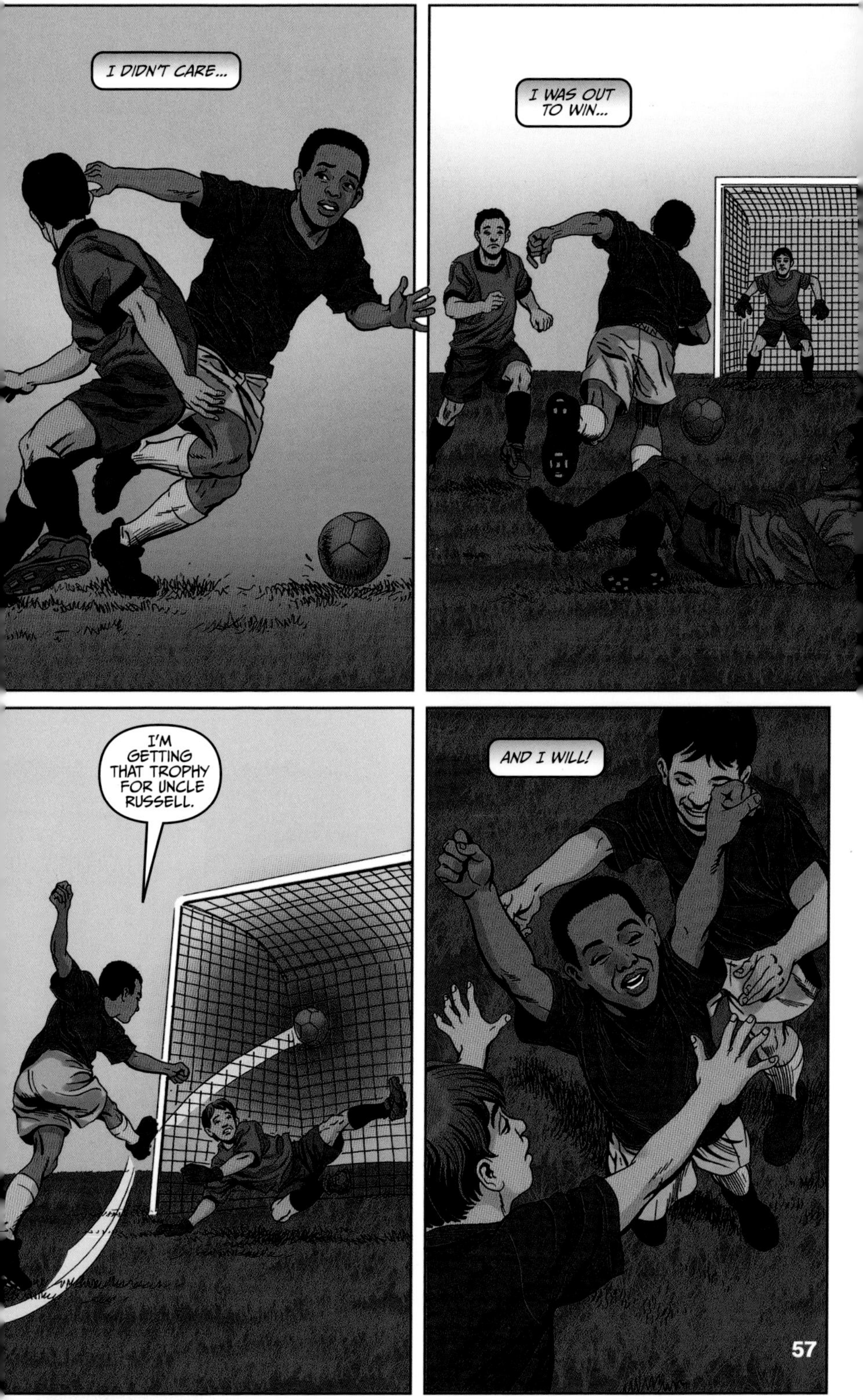
I DIDN'T CARE...
I WAS OUT TO WIN...
I'M GETTING THAT TROPHY FOR UNCLE RUSSELL.
AND I WILL!

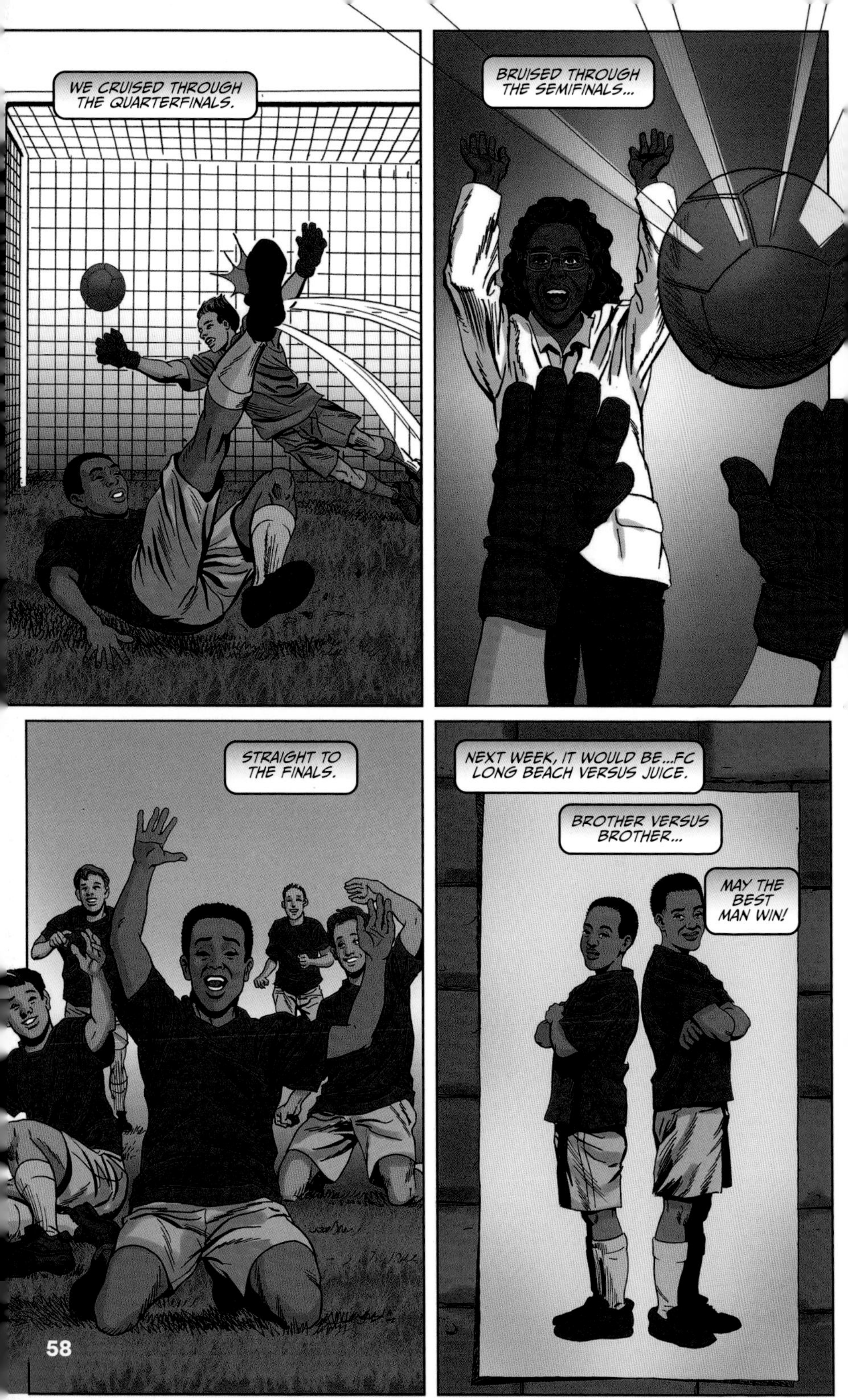
WE CRUISED THROUGH THE QUARTERFINALS.
BRUISED THROUGH THE SEMIFINALS...
STRAIGHT TO THE FINALS.
NEXT WEEK, IT WOULD BE...FC LONG BEACH VERSUS JUICE.
BROTHER VERSUS BROTHER...
MAY THE BEST MAN WIN!

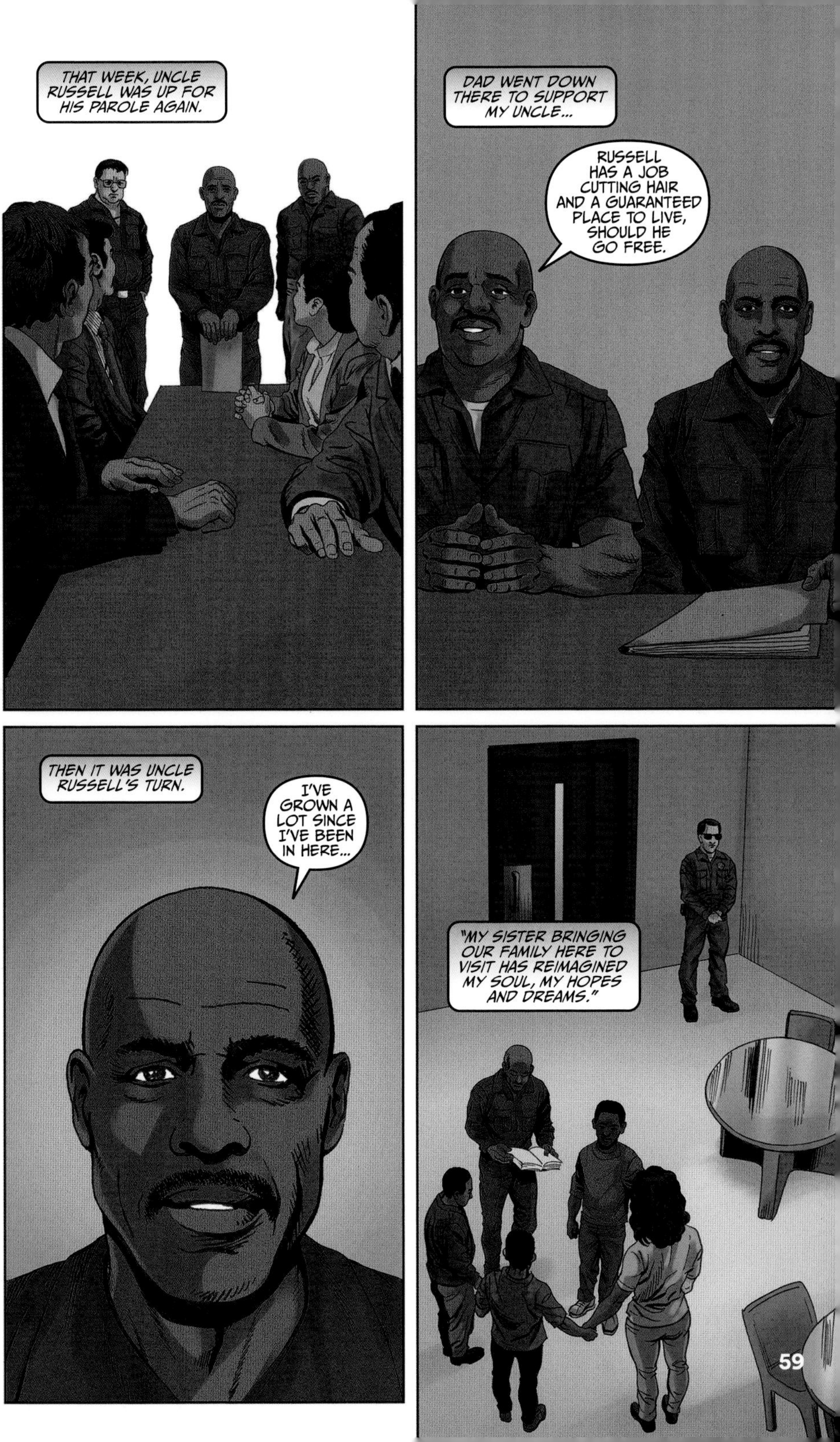
THAT WEEK, UNCLE RUSSELL WAS UP FOR HIS PAROLE AGAIN.
DAD WENT DOWN THERE TO SUPPORT MY UNCLE...
RUSSELL HAS A JOB CUTTING HAIR AND A GUARANTEED PLACE TO LIVE, SHOULD HE GO FREE.
THEN IT WAS UNCLE RUSSELL'S TURN.
I'VE GROWN A LOT SINCE I'VE BEEN IN HERE...
"MY SISTER BRINGING OUR FAMILY HERE TO VISIT HAS REIMAGINED MY SOUL, MY HOPES AND DREAMS."

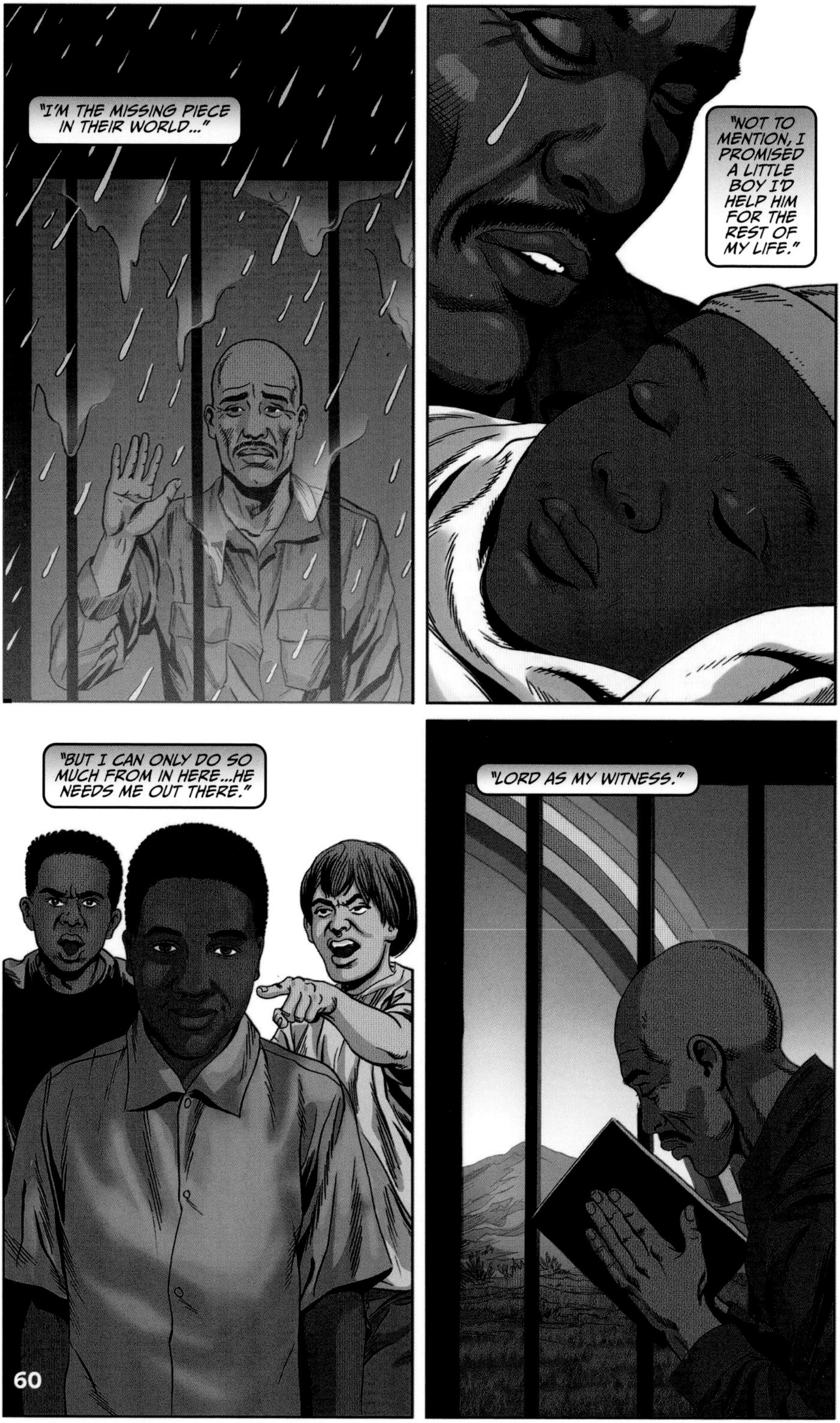
"I'M THE MISSING PIECE IN THEIR WORLD..."
"NOT TO MENTION, I PROMISED A LITTLE BOY I'D HELP HIM FOR THE REST OF MY LIFE."
"BUT I CAN ONLY DO SO MUCH FROM IN HERE...HE NEEDS ME OUT THERE."
"LORD AS MY WITNESS."

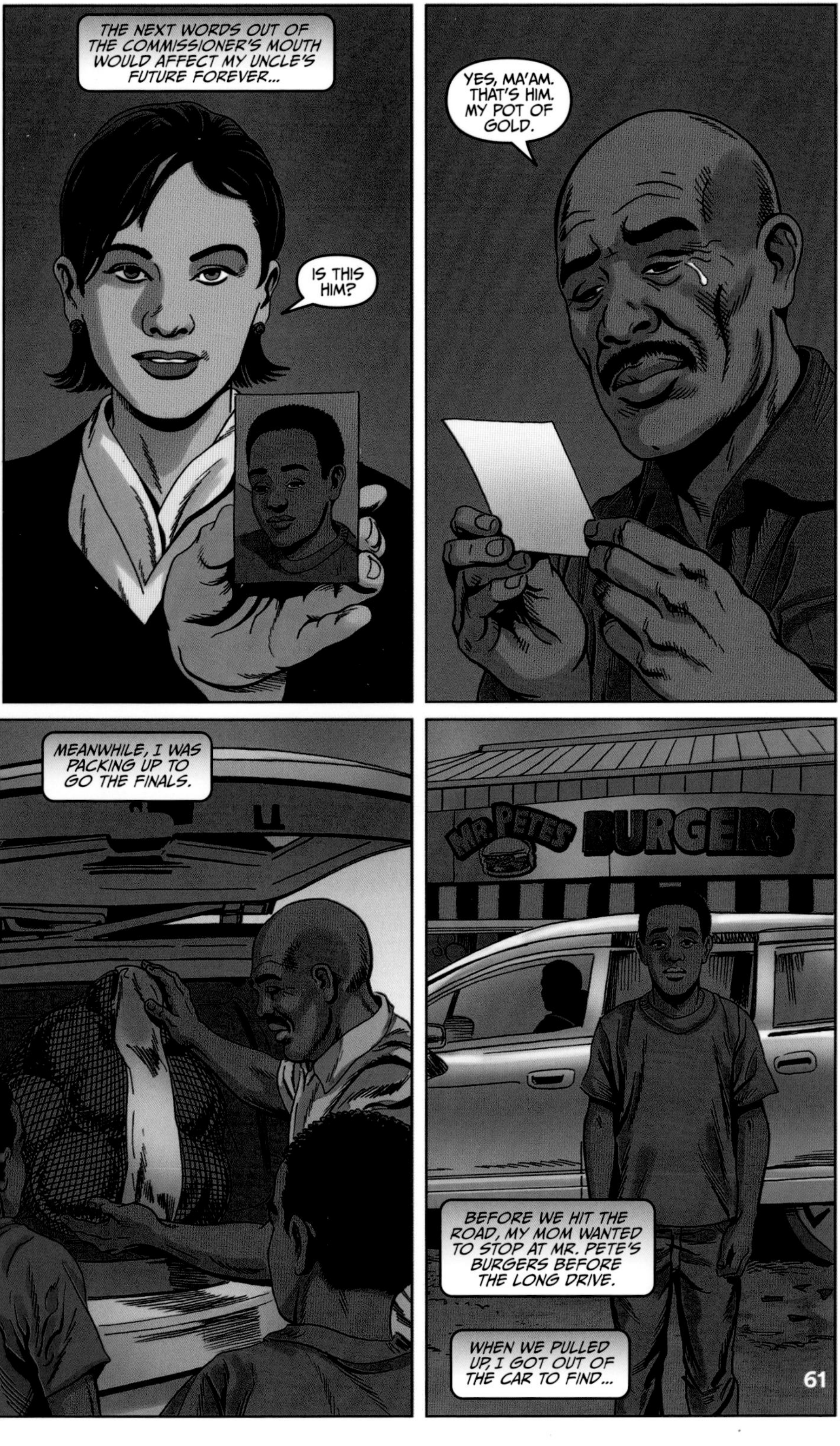
THE NEXT WORDS OUT OF THE COMMISSIONER'S MOUTH WOULD AFFECT MY UNCLE'S FUTURE FOREVER...
IS THIS HIM?
YES, MA'AM. THAT'S HIM. MY POT OF GOLD.
MEANWHILE, I WAS PACKING UP TO GO THE FINALS.
MR. PETE'S BURGERS
BEFORE WE HIT THE ROAD, MY MOM WANTED TO STOP AT MR. PETE'S BURGERS BEFORE THE LONG DRIVE.
WHEN WE PULLED UP, I GOT OUT OF THE CAR TO FIND...

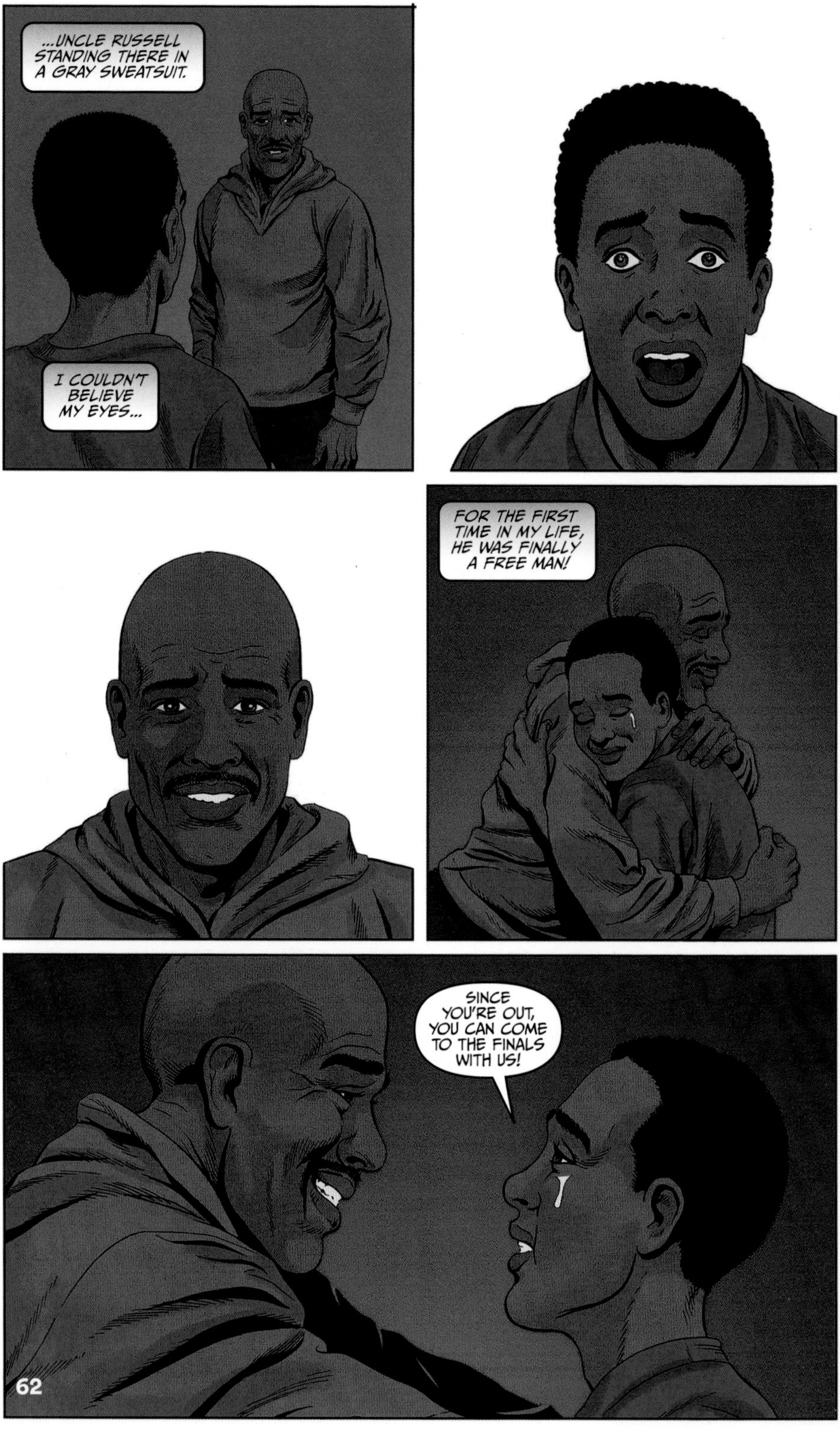
...UNCLE RUSSELL STANDING THERE IN A GRAY SWEATSUIT.
I COULDN'T BELIEVE MY EYES...
FOR THE FIRST TIME IN MY LIFE, HE WAS FINALLY A FREE MAN!
SINCE YOU'RE OUT, YOU CAN COME TO THE FINALS WITH US!

I CAN'T TRAVEL MORE THAN 25 MILES FROM MY HOME, AND SAN DIEGO'S 120 MILES AWAY.

THAT'S NOT FAIR! YOU'RE FREE!

I'M AS FREE AS A FREE BLACK MAN CAN BE...NOW ALL I NEED YOU TO DO IS ONE THING...

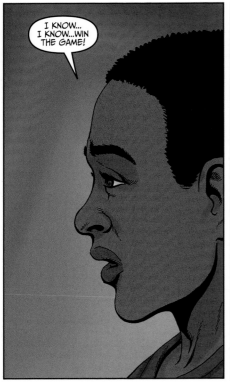

I KNOW... I KNOW...WIN THE GAME!

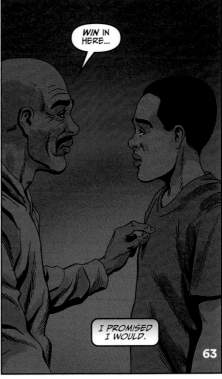

WIN IN HERE...

I PROMISED I WOULD.

63

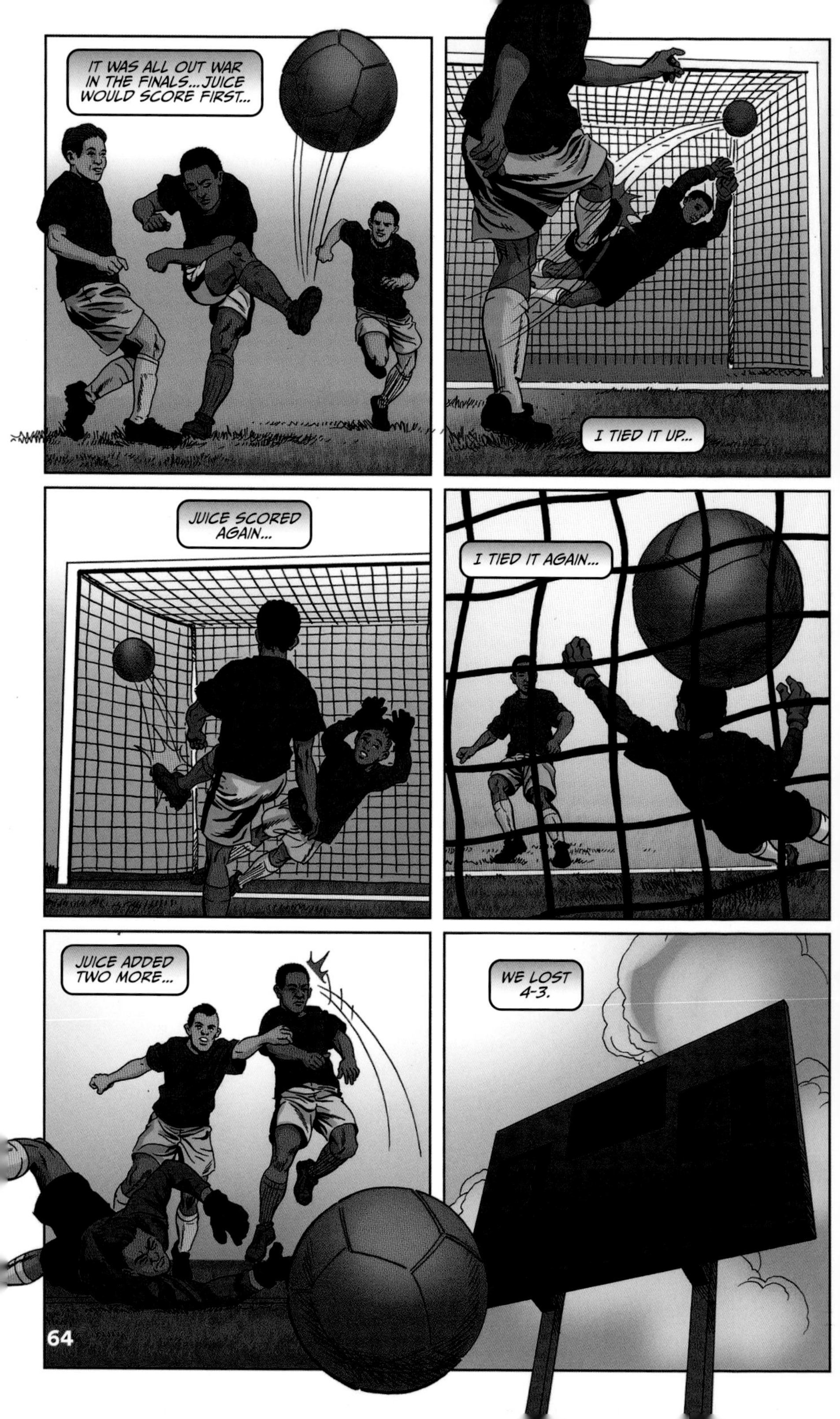
IT WAS ALL OUT WAR IN THE FINALS... JUICE WOULD SCORE FIRST...
I TIED IT UP...
JUICE SCORED AGAIN...
I TIED IT AGAIN...
JUICE ADDED TWO MORE...
WE LOST 4-3.

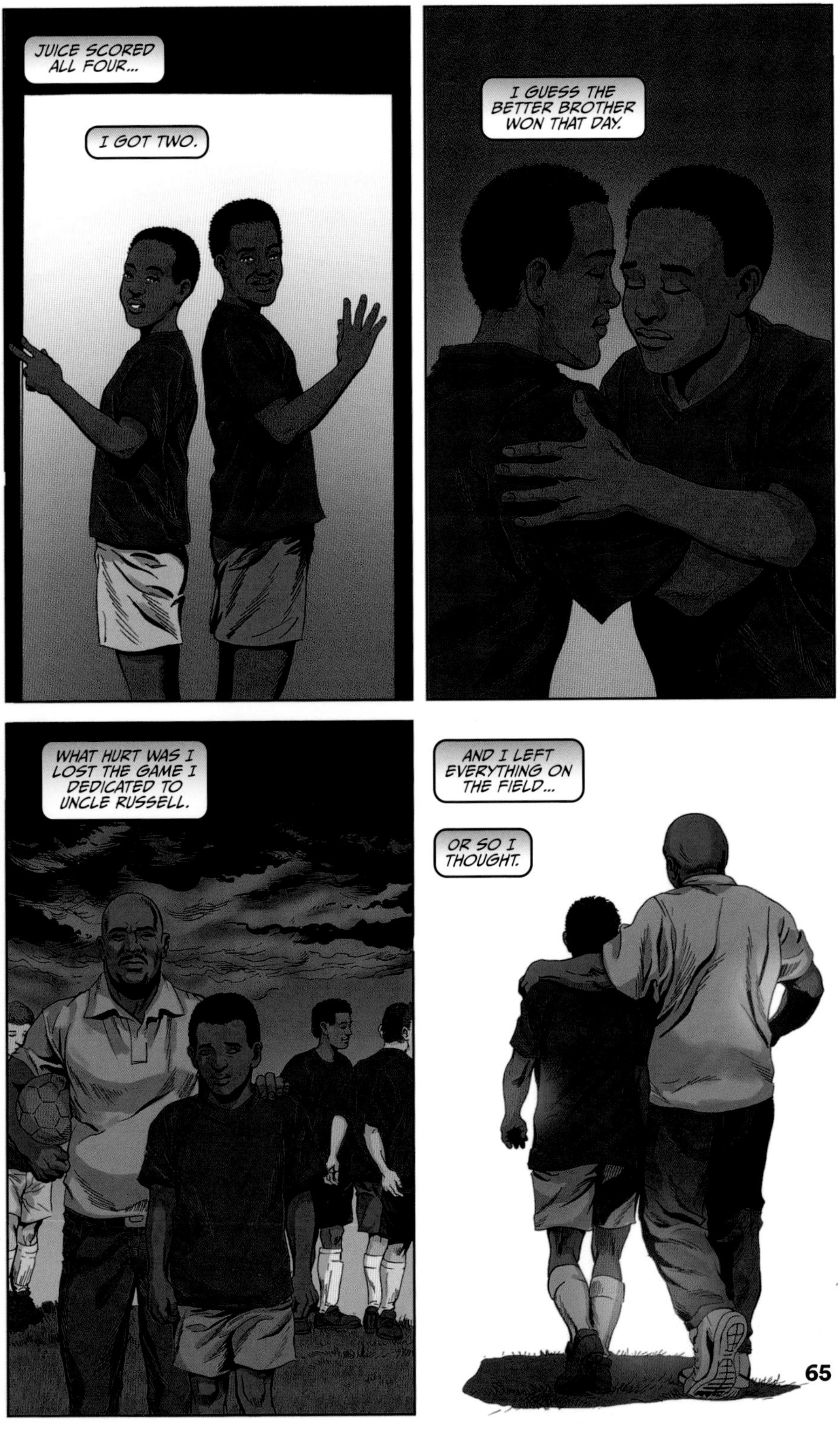
JUICE SCORED ALL FOUR...
I GOT TWO.
I GUESS THE BETTER BROTHER WON THAT DAY.
WHAT HURT WAS I LOST THE GAME I DEDICATED TO UNCLE RUSSELL.
AND I LEFT EVERYTHING ON THE FIELD...
OR SO I THOUGHT.

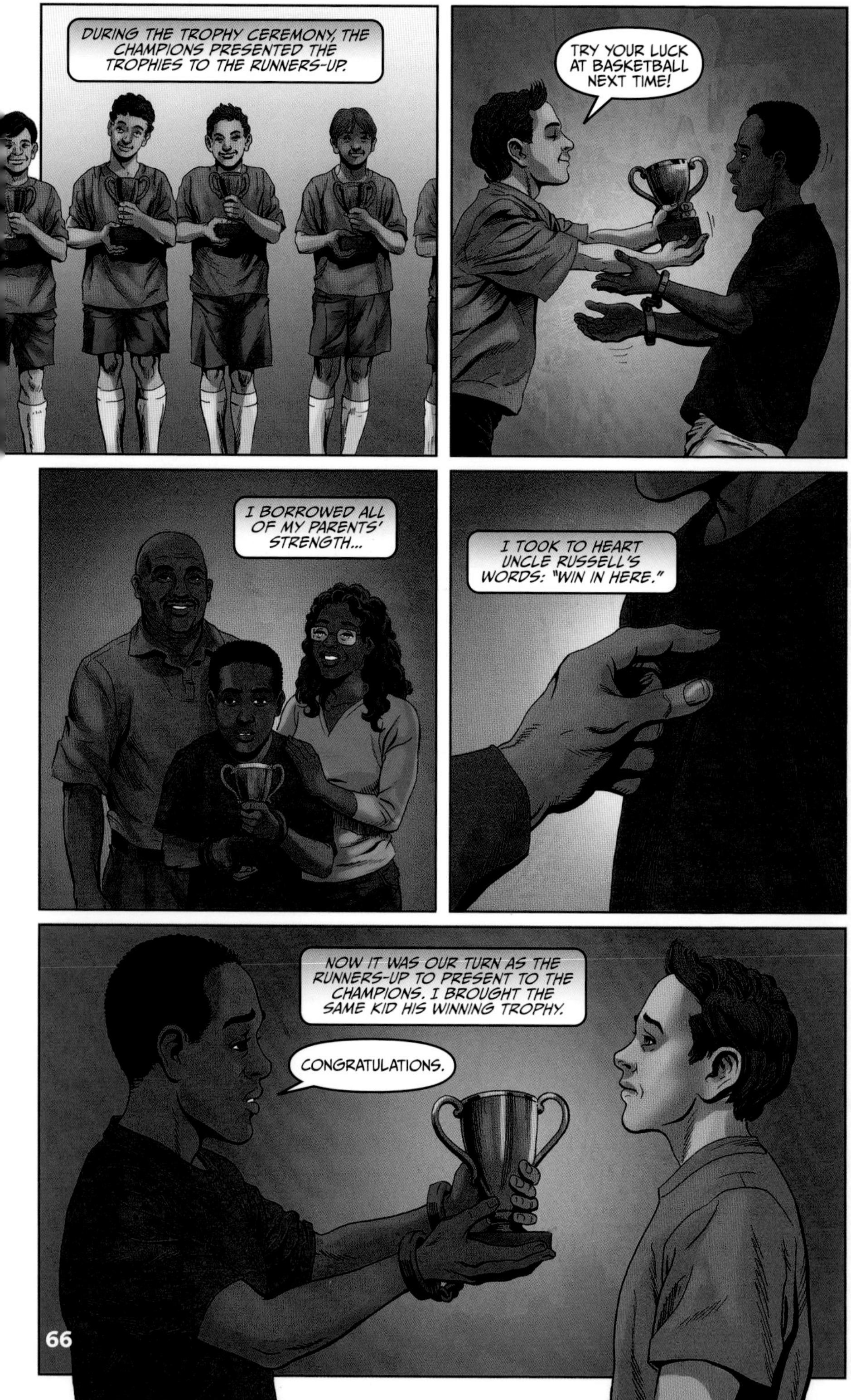
DURING THE TROPHY CEREMONY, THE CHAMPIONS PRESENTED THE TROPHIES TO THE RUNNERS-UP.
TRY YOUR LUCK AT BASKETBALL NEXT TIME!
I BORROWED ALL OF MY PARENTS' STRENGTH...
I TOOK TO HEART UNCLE RUSSELL'S WORDS: "WIN IN HERE."
NOW IT WAS OUR TURN AS THE RUNNERS-UP TO PRESENT TO THE CHAMPIONS. I BROUGHT THE SAME KID HIS WINNING TROPHY.
CONGRATULATIONS.

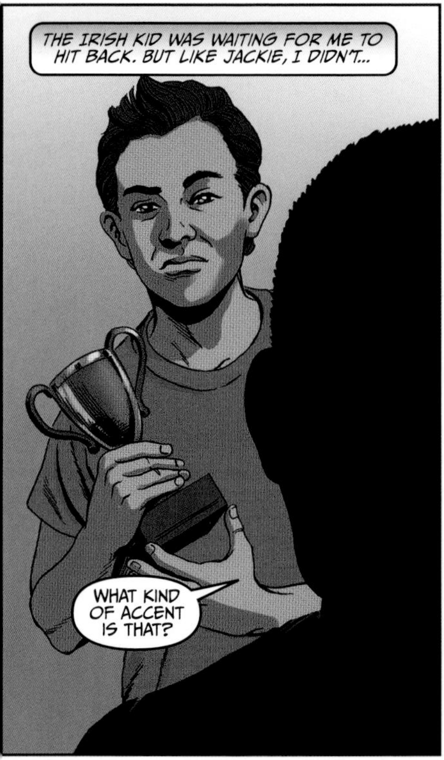
THE IRISH KID WAS WAITING FOR ME TO HIT BACK. BUT LIKE JACKIE, I DIDN'T...
WHAT KIND OF ACCENT IS THAT?

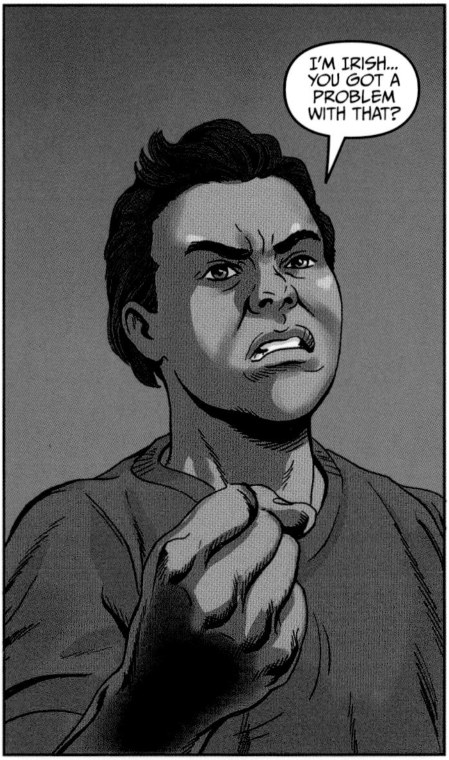
I'M IRISH... YOU GOT A PROBLEM WITH THAT?

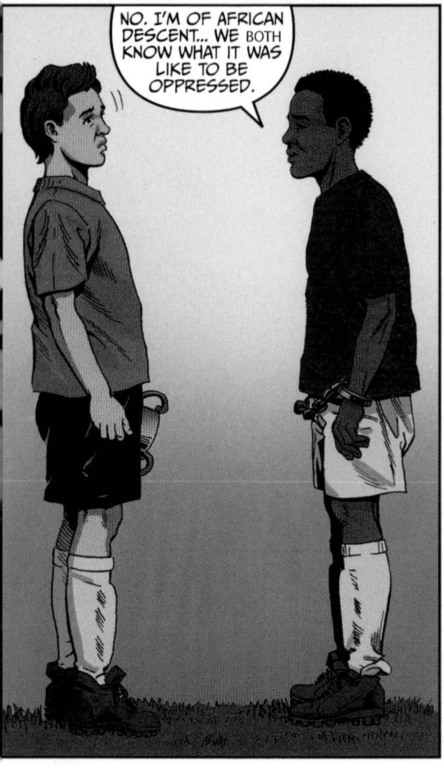
NO. I'M OF AFRICAN DESCENT... WE BOTH KNOW WHAT IT WAS LIKE TO BE OPPRESSED.

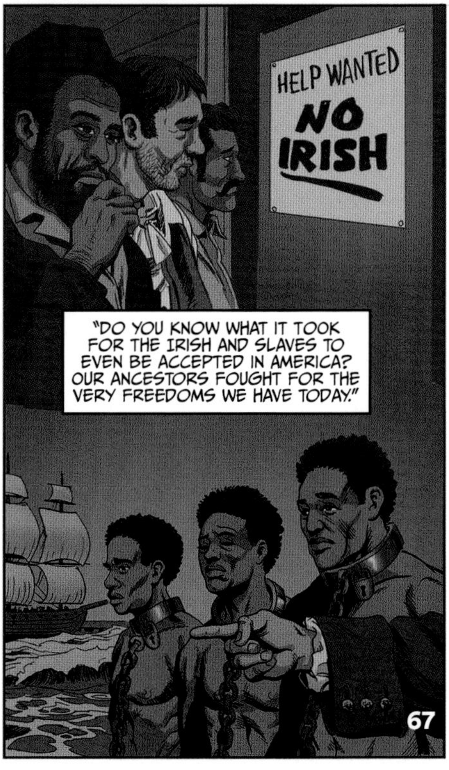
HELP WANTED
NO IRISH
"DO YOU KNOW WHAT IT TOOK FOR THE IRISH AND SLAVES TO EVEN BE ACCEPTED IN AMERICA? OUR ANCESTORS FOUGHT FOR THE VERY FREEDOMS WE HAVE TODAY."

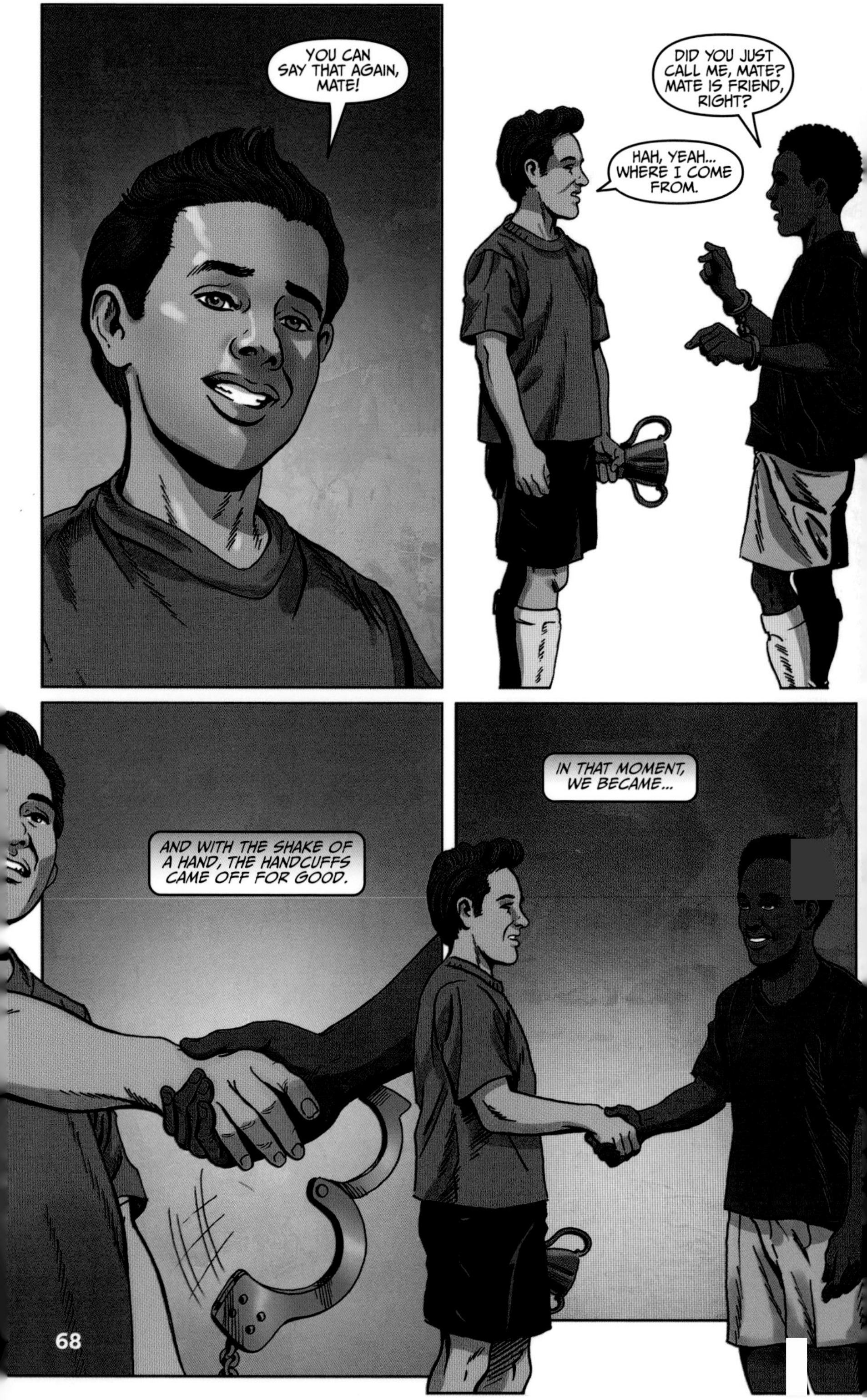
YOU CAN SAY THAT AGAIN, MATE!
DID YOU JUST CALL ME, MATE? MATE IS FRIEND, RIGHT?
HAH, YEAH... WHERE I COME FROM.
AND WITH THE SHAKE OF A HAND, THE HANDCUFFS CAME OFF FOR GOOD.
IN THAT MOMENT, WE BECAME...

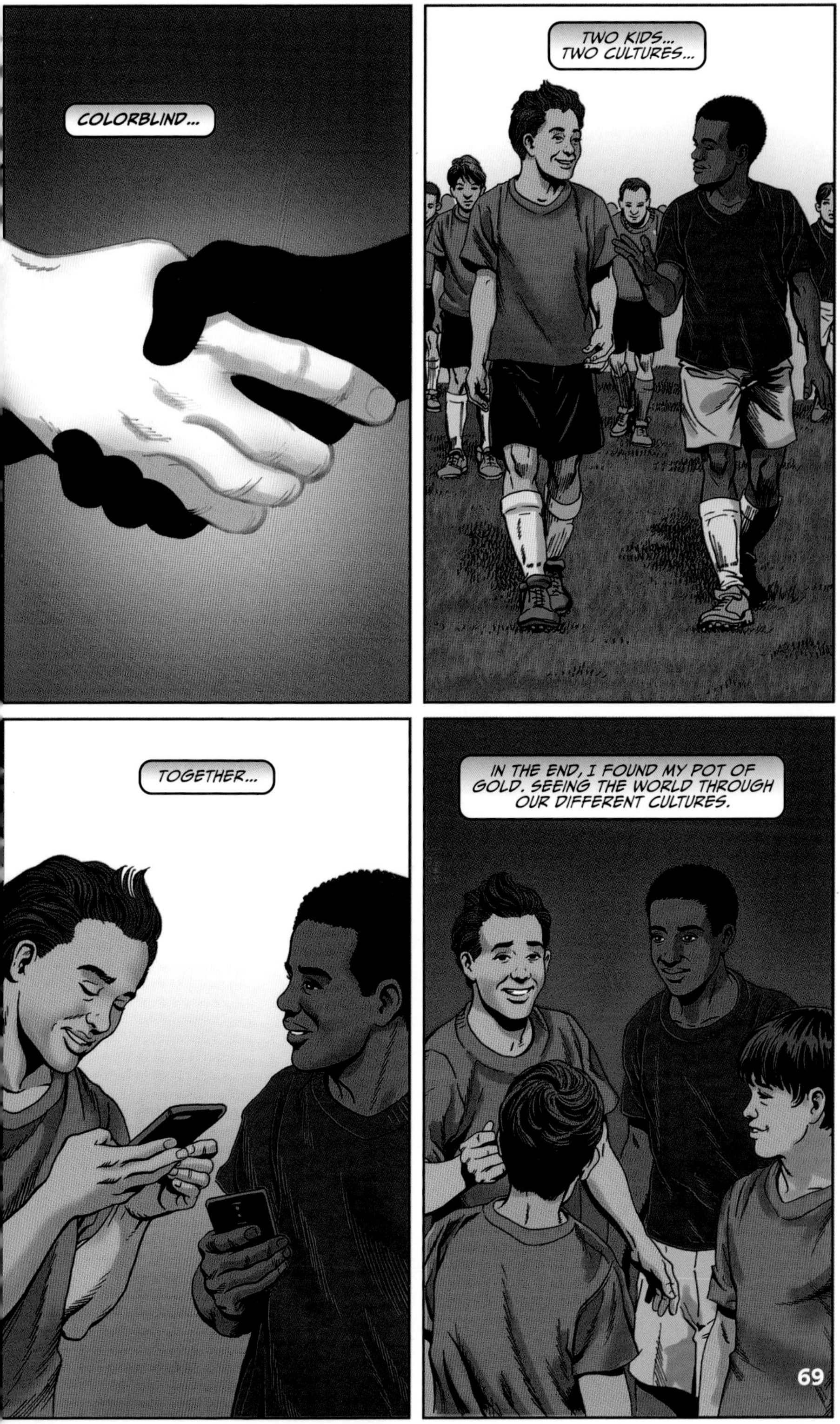
COLORBLIND...
TWO KIDS... TWO CULTURES...
TOGETHER...
IN THE END, I FOUND MY POT OF GOLD. SEEING THE WORLD THROUGH OUR DIFFERENT CULTURES.

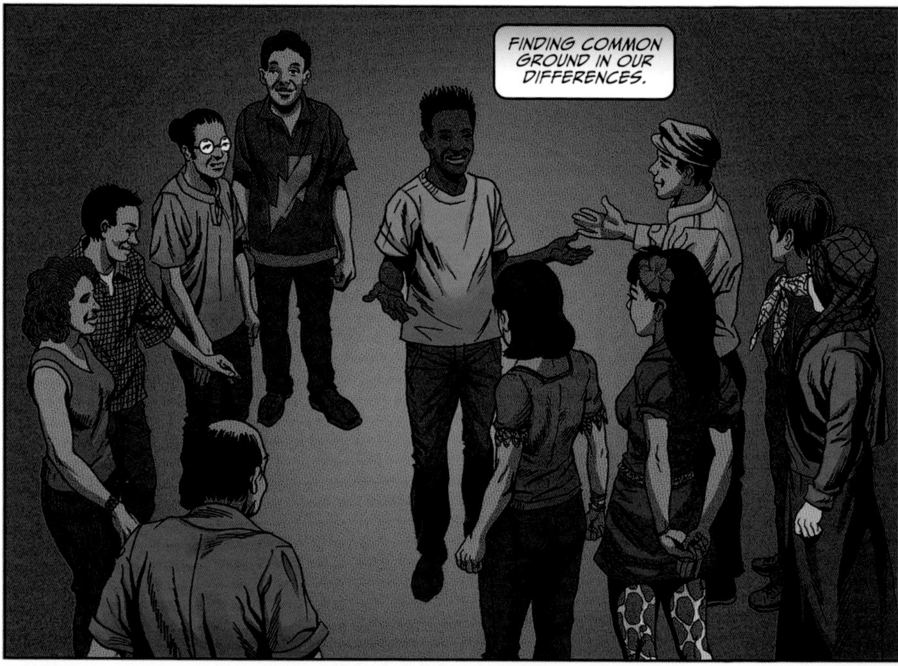
FINDING COMMON GROUND IN OUR DIFFERENCES.

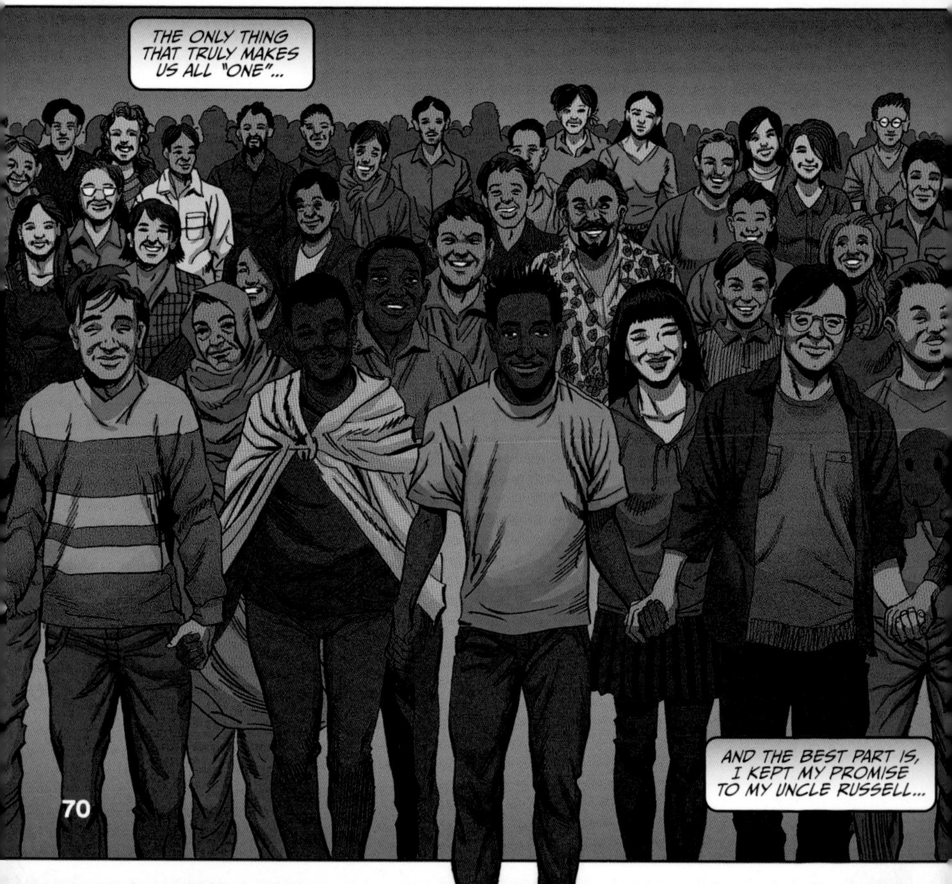
THE ONLY THING THAT TRULY MAKES US ALL "ONE"...
AND THE BEST PART IS, I KEPT MY PROMISE TO MY UNCLE RUSSELL...

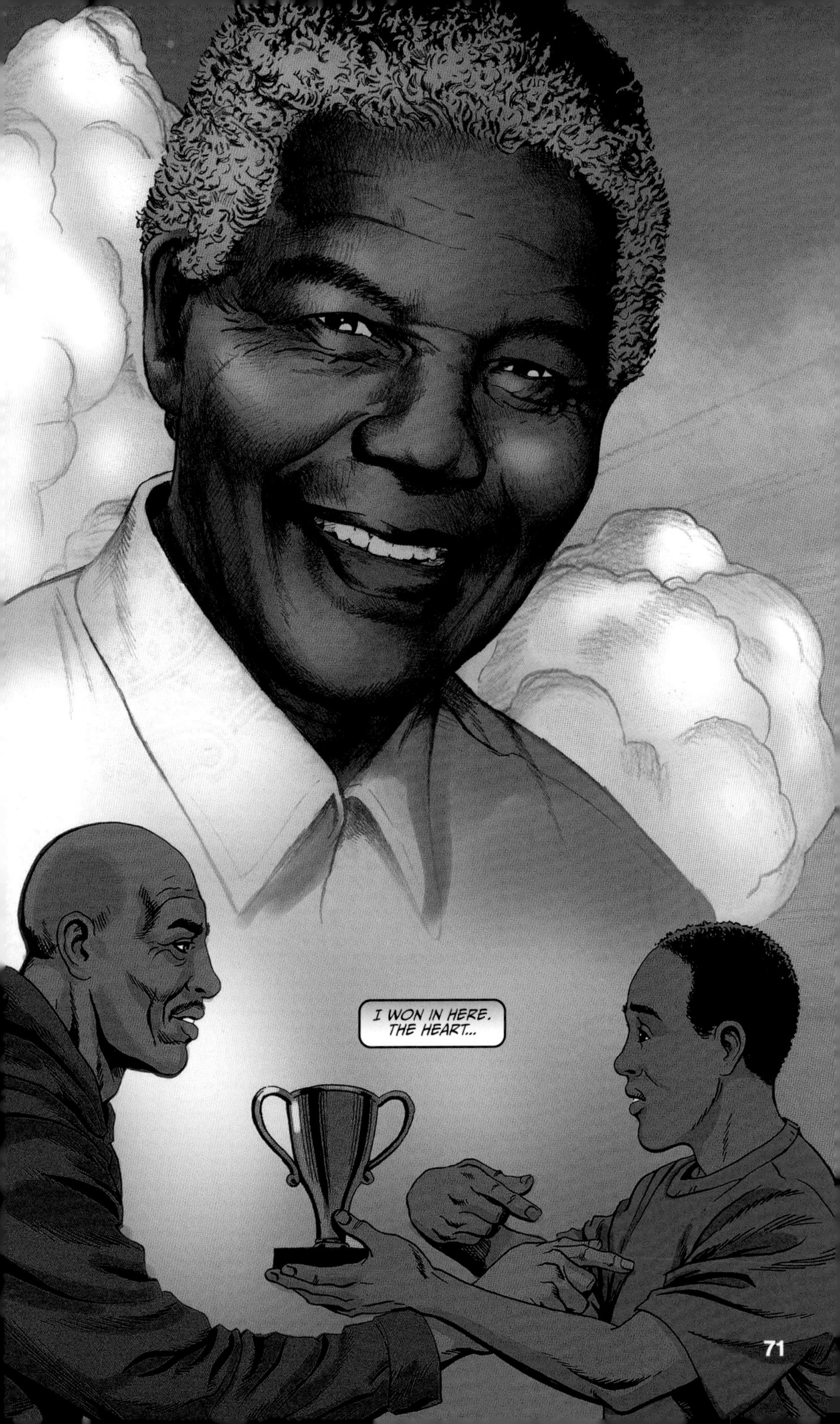
I WON IN HERE. THE HEART...

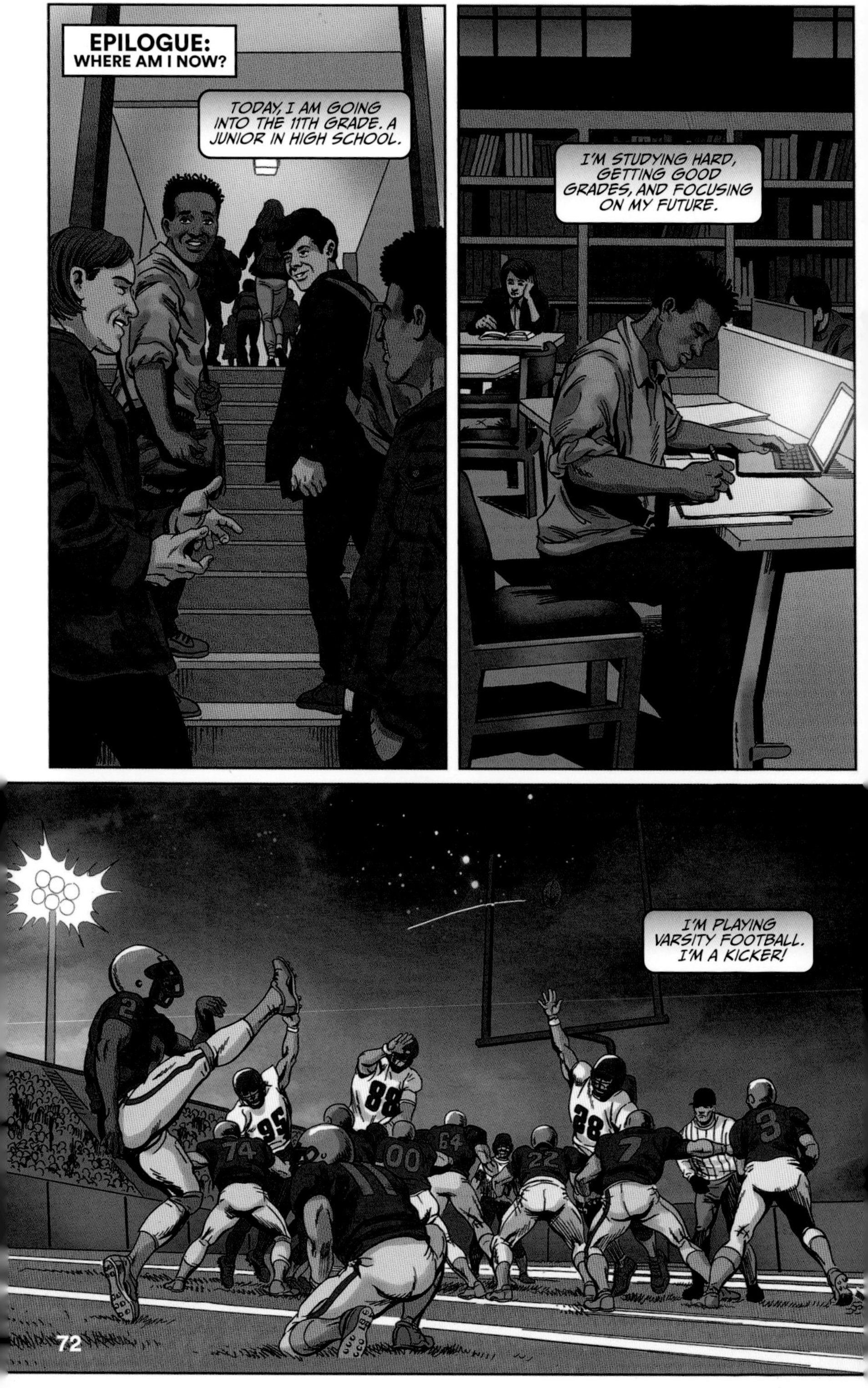
EPILOGUE:
WHERE AM I NOW?
TODAY, I AM GOING INTO THE 11TH GRADE. A JUNIOR IN HIGH SCHOOL.
I'M STUDYING HARD, GETTING GOOD GRADES, AND FOCUSING ON MY FUTURE.
I'M PLAYING VARSITY FOOTBALL. I'M A KICKER!

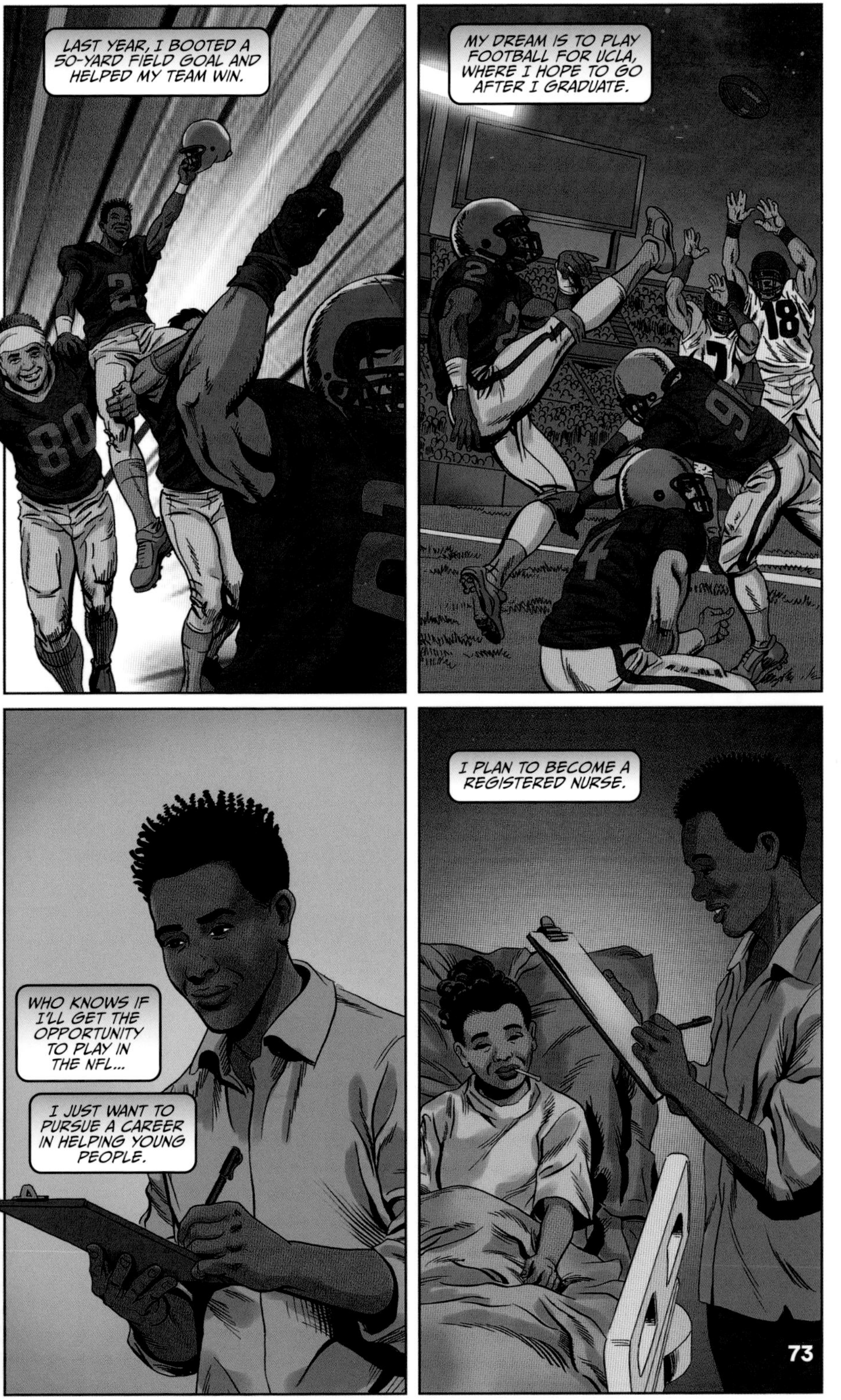
LAST YEAR, I BOOTED A 50-YARD FIELD GOAL AND HELPED MY TEAM WIN.
MY DREAM IS TO PLAY FOOTBALL FOR UCLA, WHERE I HOPE TO GO AFTER I GRADUATE.
WHO KNOWS IF I'LL GET THE OPPORTUNITY TO PLAY IN THE NFL...
I JUST WANT TO PURSUE A CAREER IN HELPING YOUNG PEOPLE.
I PLAN TO BECOME A REGISTERED NURSE.

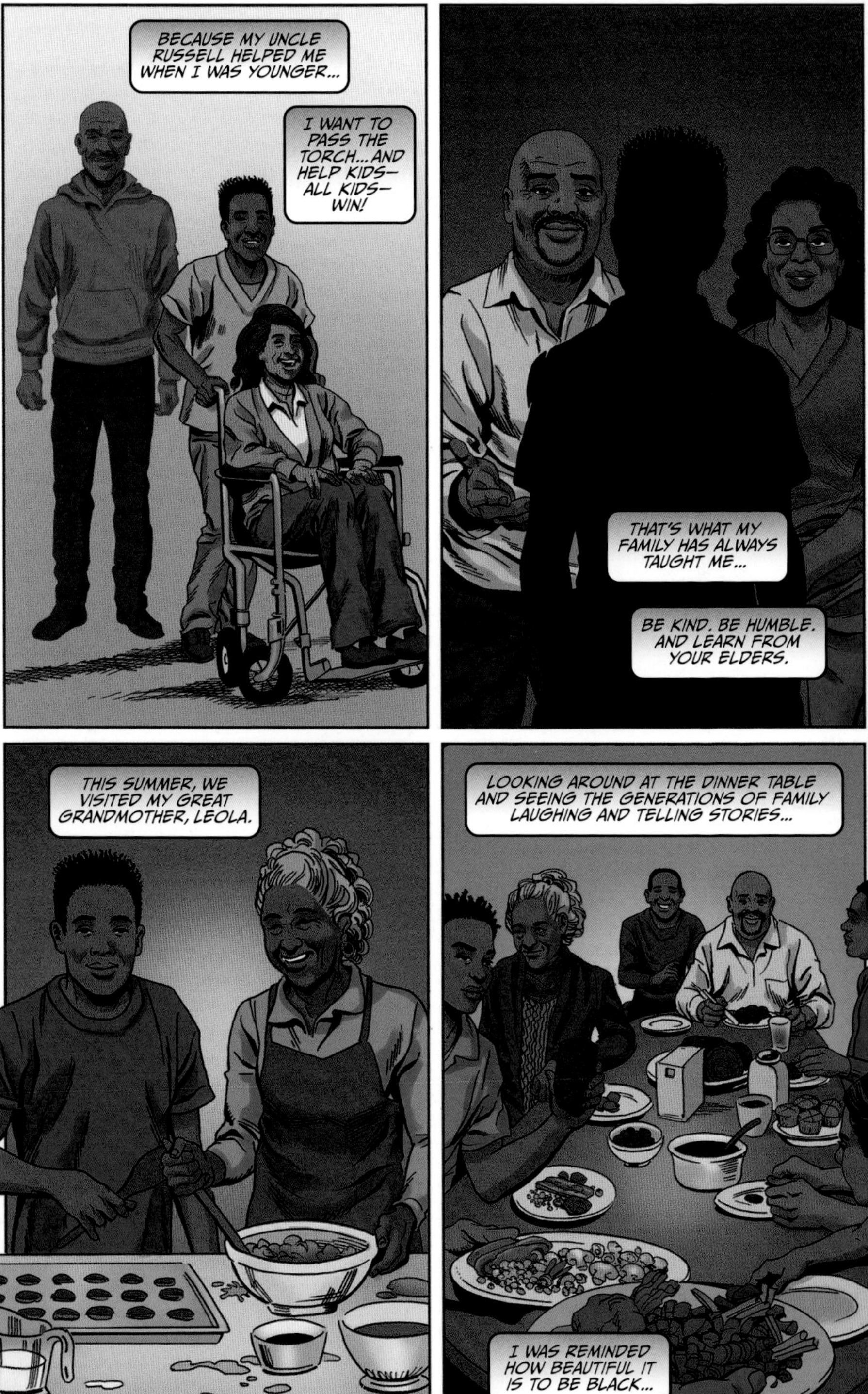

BECAUSE MY UNCLE RUSSELL HELPED ME WHEN I WAS YOUNGER...
I WANT TO PASS THE TORCH...AND HELP KIDS—ALL KIDS—WIN!
THAT'S WHAT MY FAMILY HAS ALWAYS TAUGHT ME...
BE KIND. BE HUMBLE. AND LEARN FROM YOUR ELDERS.
THIS SUMMER, WE VISITED MY GREAT GRANDMOTHER, LEOLA.
LOOKING AROUND AT THE DINNER TABLE AND SEEING THE GENERATIONS OF FAMILY LAUGHING AND TELLING STORIES...
I WAS REMINDED HOW BEAUTIFUL IT IS TO BE BLACK...

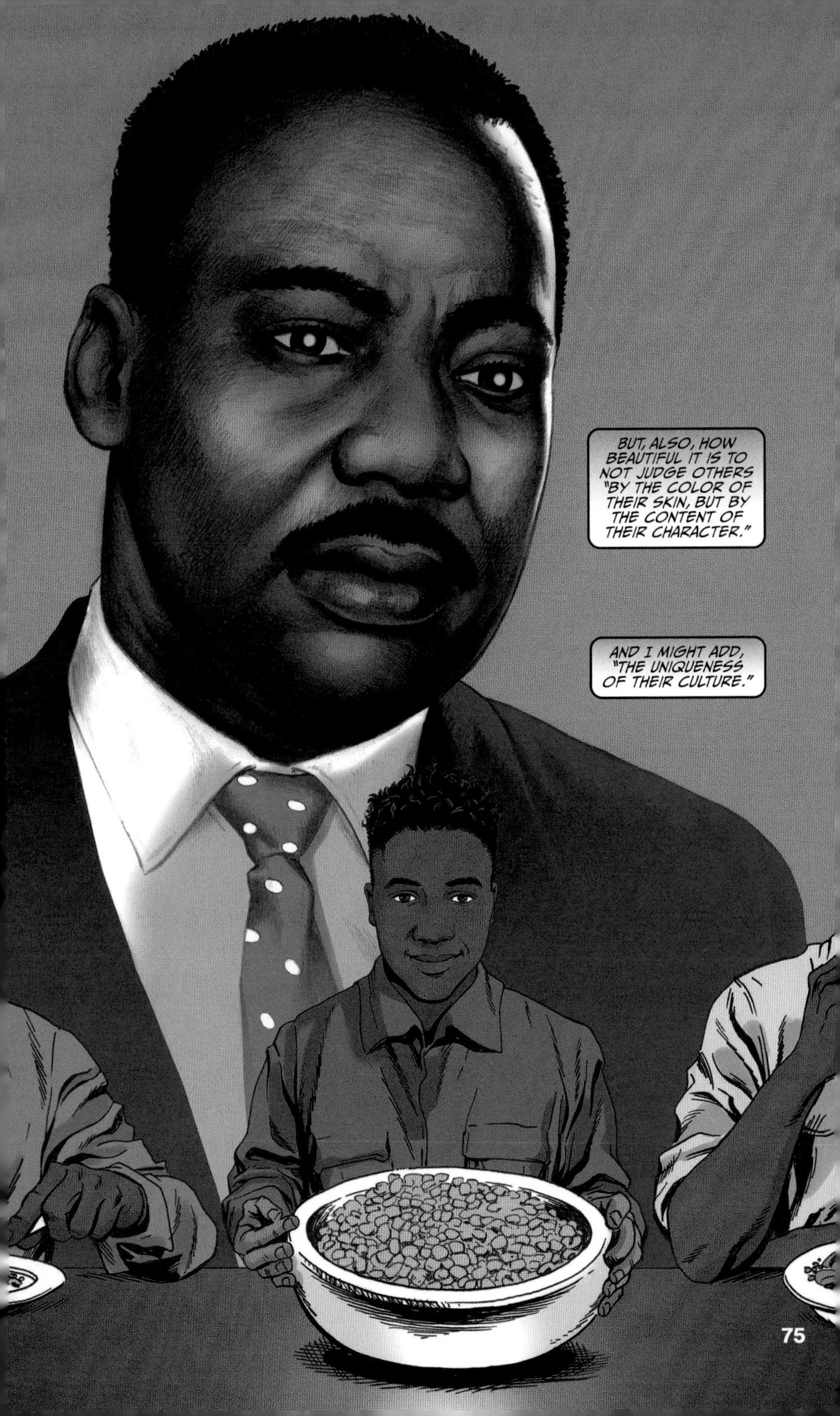
BUT, ALSO, HOW BEAUTIFUL IT IS TO NOT JUDGE OTHERS "BY THE COLOR OF THEIR SKIN, BUT BY THE CONTENT OF THEIR CHARACTER."
AND I MIGHT ADD, "THE UNIQUENESS OF THEIR CULTURE."

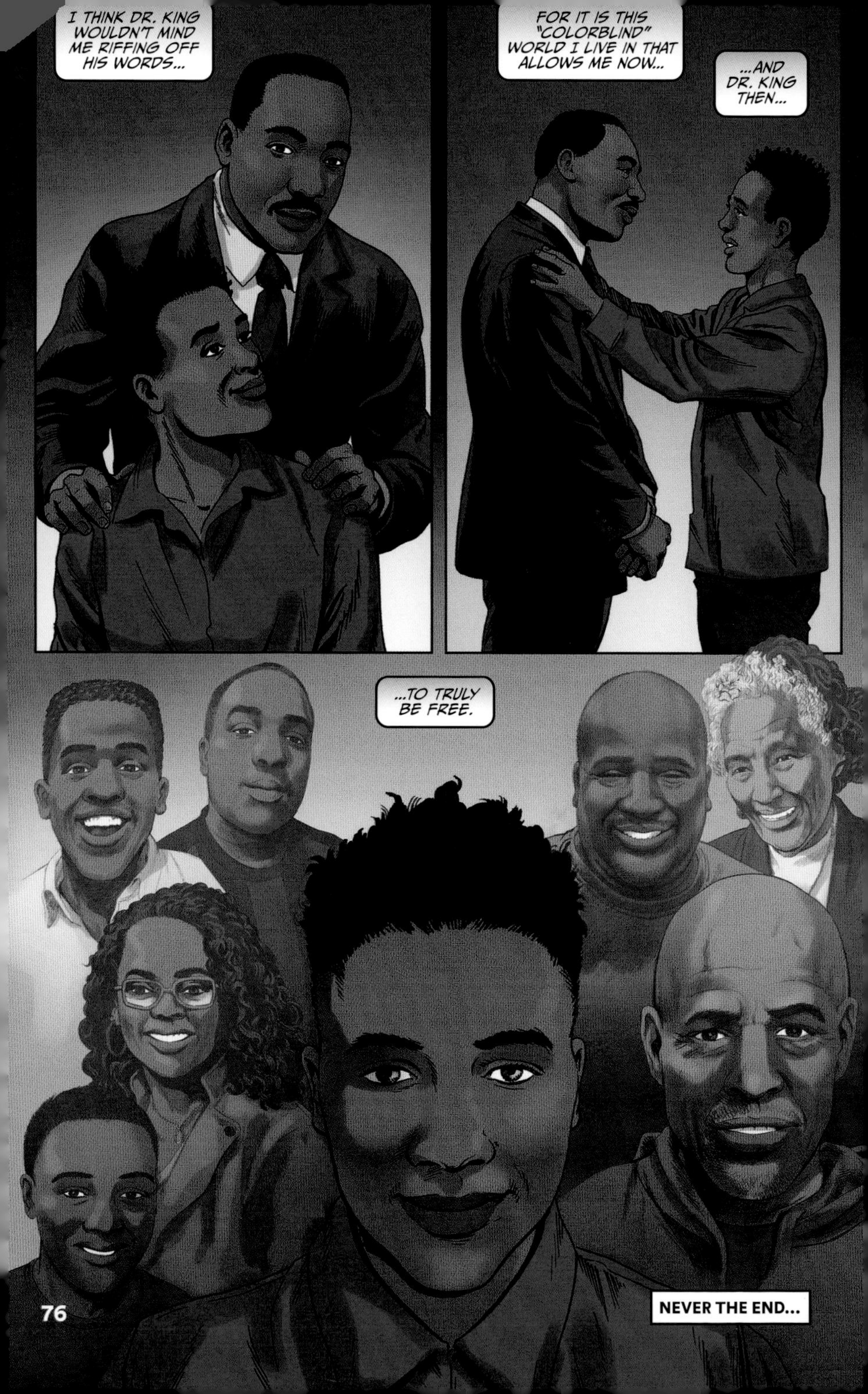
I THINK DR. KING WOULDN'T MIND ME RIFFING OFF HIS WORDS...
FOR IT IS THIS "COLORBLIND" WORLD I LIVE IN THAT ALLOWS ME NOW...
...AND DR. KING THEN...
...TO TRULY BE FREE.
NEVER THE END...

ABOUT OUR AUTHOR

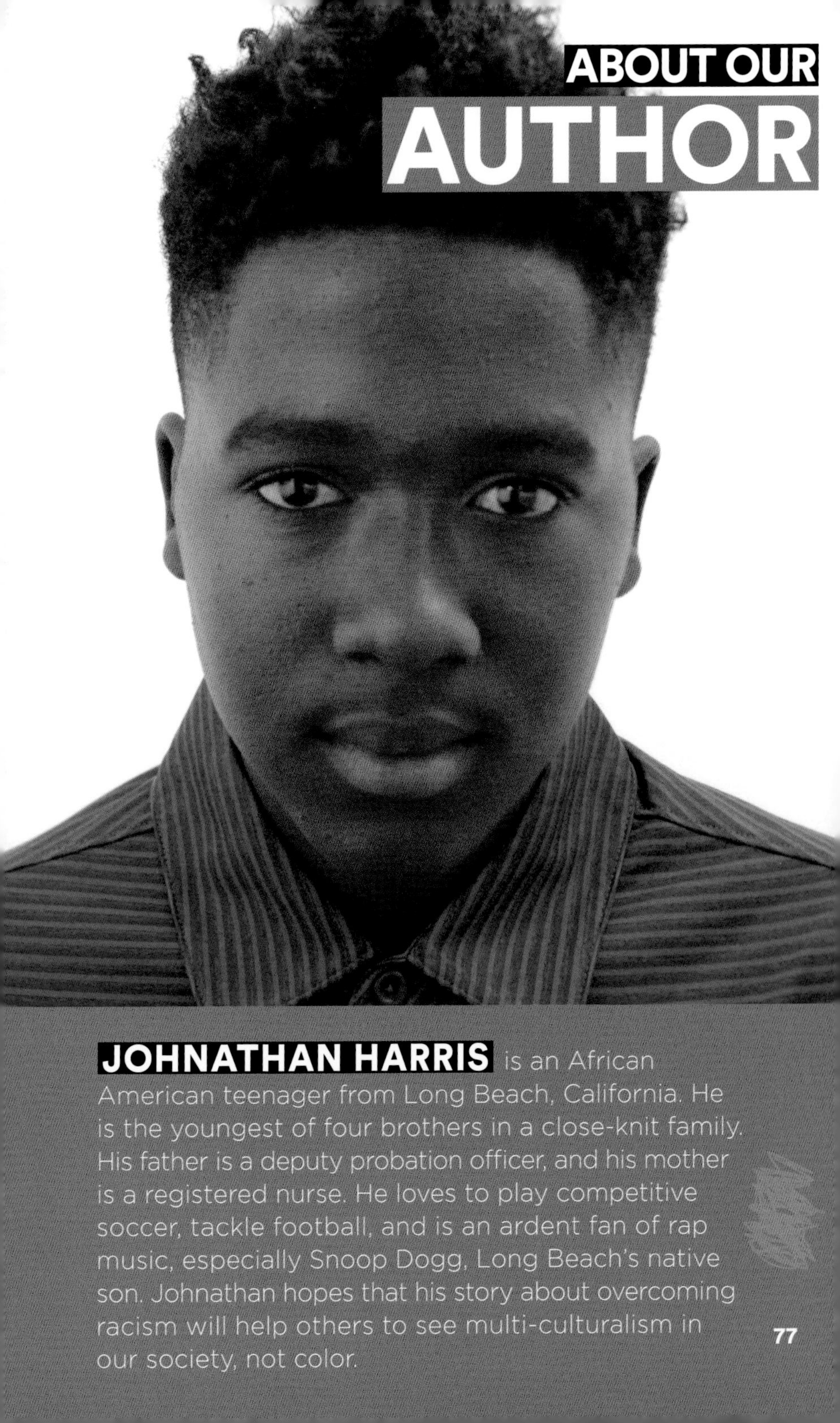

JOHNATHAN HARRIS is an African American teenager from Long Beach, California. He is the youngest of four brothers in a close-knit family. His father is a deputy probation officer, and his mother is a registered nurse. He loves to play competitive soccer, tackle football, and is an ardent fan of rap music, especially Snoop Dogg, Long Beach's native son. Johnathan hopes that his story about overcoming racism will help others to see multi-culturalism in our society, not color.

JOHNATHAN...

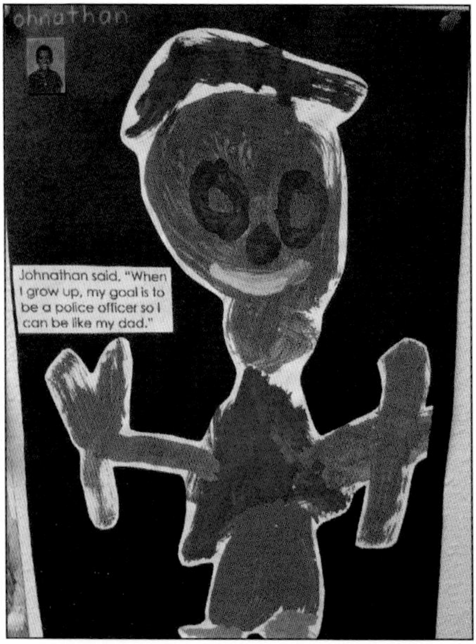
Johnathan said, "When I grow up, my goal is to be a police officer so I can be like my dad."

Artwork from kindergarten. I wanted to be a police officer like my dad.

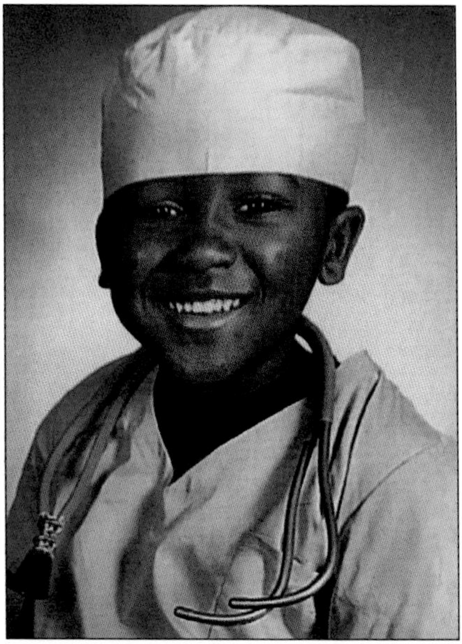

Did anyone call a nurse? I'm here . . .

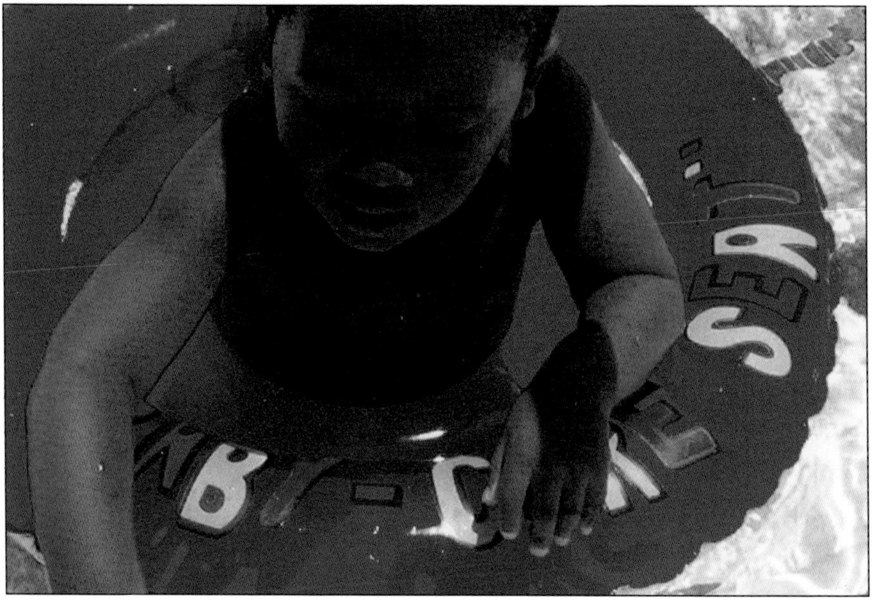

Just floating through life at 3-years-old. Me, on our yearly trip to Palm Springs.

JOHNATHAN...

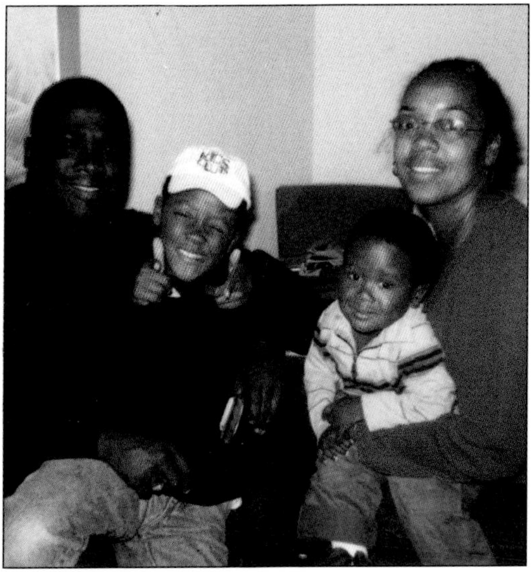

This is a picture of my mom, dad, and brother visiting Uncle Russell in prison.

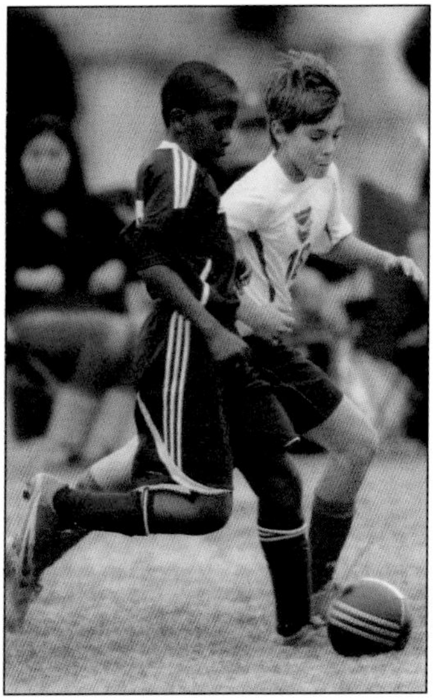

This is the State Cup when I played for FC Long Beach.

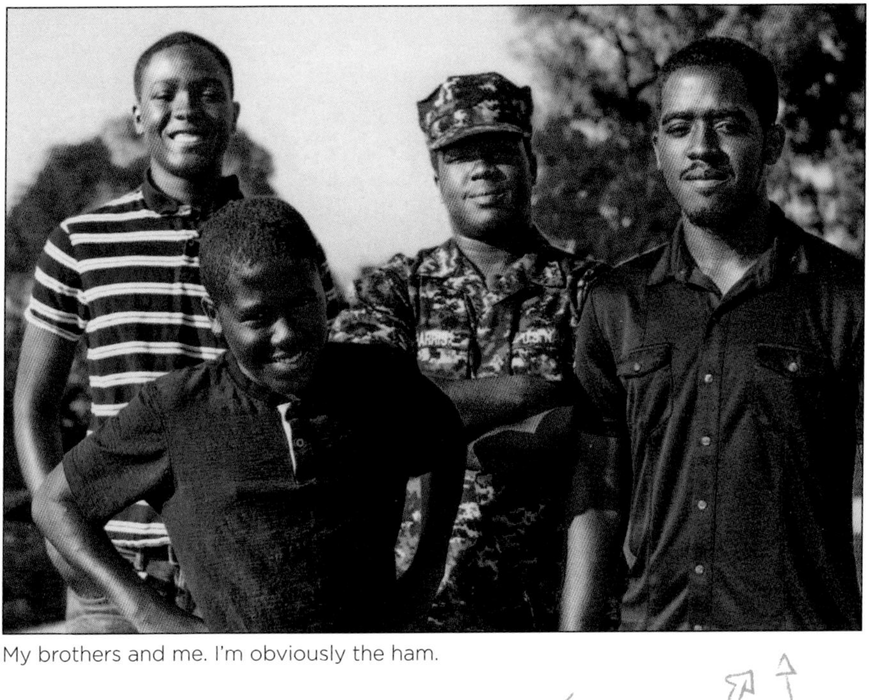

My brothers and me. I'm obviously the ham.

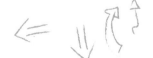

JOHNATHAN...

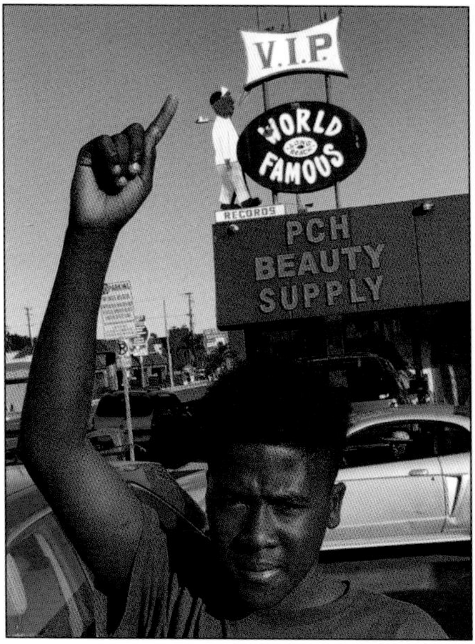
V.I.P.
WORLD FAMOUS
RECORDS
PCH
BEAUTY
SUPPLY
This is me in front of the famous VIP Records in Long Beach, CA.

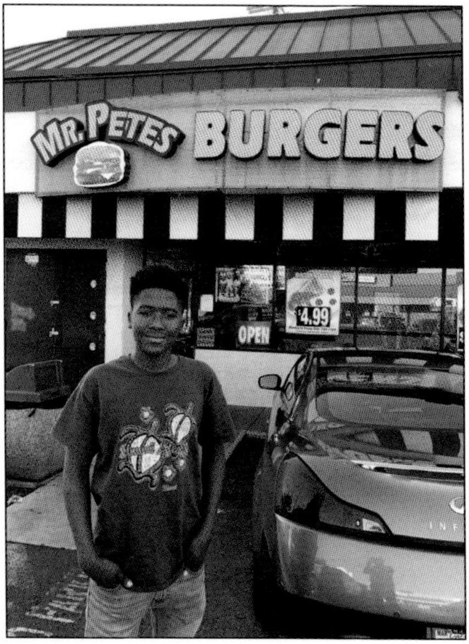
MR. PETES
BURGERS
OPEN
$4.99
Mr. Pete's Burgers. This is where Uncle Russell surprised me. A free man at last!

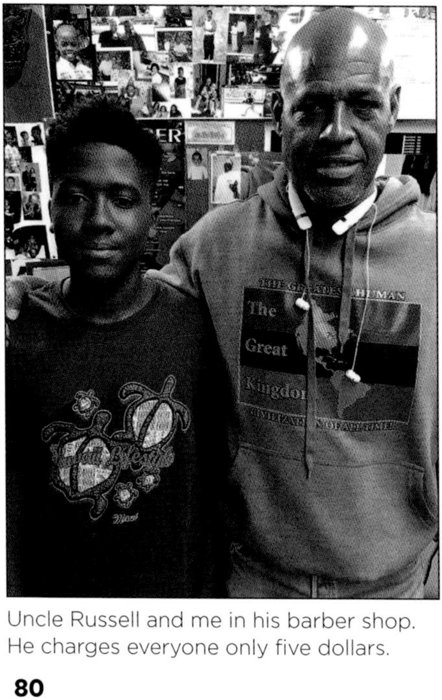
The
Great
Uncle Russell and me in his barber shop. He charges everyone only five dollars.

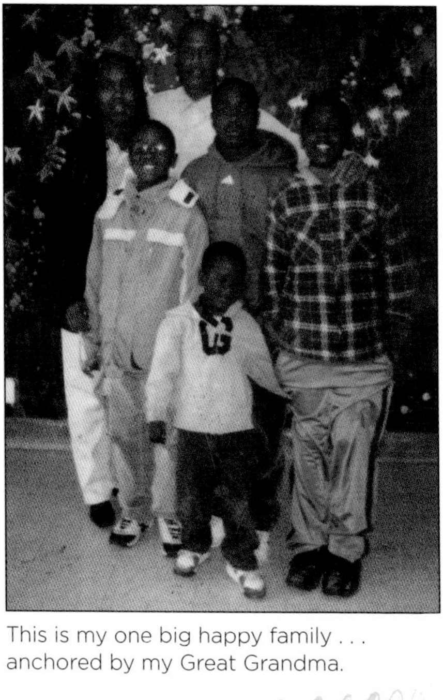
This is my one big happy family . . . anchored by my Great Grandma.

TAKE 5!

FIVE PARENT TAKE-AWAYS ABOUT RACISM

ROBERT W. CLARK

Robert W. Clark is a Former Senior FBI Official who served as the Assistant Special Agent in Charge for the city of Los Angeles. After a 30-year career, Mr. Clark oversaw various criminal programs for the FBI, including the Gang and Violent Crime Units.

CULTURE, NOT SKIN COLOR, MATTERS MOST.

America is a melting pot of cultures. It's what makes our country so great. In order to truly honor each other, we must embrace and take a genuine interest in our various backgrounds. Our differences provide the foundation upon which every man, woman, and child can be equal.

THERE ARE GOOD COPS AND BAD COPS, BUT MOSTLY GREAT COPS.

Law enforcement is a tough job. It is not until you walk in the shoes of a police officer that you can truly understand the complexity and dangers involved in keeping civilians safe. In my 30-year career, I've found one immutable truth: Most people in law enforcement are great at what they do. It's not a money job. It's a calling and passion for service.

IF YOU DO NOT WANT YOUR KIDS TO GROW UP ANGRY, LISTEN WITH A KIND AND PATIENT HEART.

It's no secret racism still plays a significant role in our country. Parents, speak with your children about their daily lives. If something hurts their feelings, listen and teach them to "lead with patient love" and to find effective ways of dealing with the world.

SOCIAL MEDIA IS WHERE A LOT OF FIRES START.

We all know the big three social media sites. For parents, my strong suggestion is that you know the passwords and monitor what your children are consuming and serving on social media. Be "friends" with them on social media so you can be engaged in what they are posting. Young people are more apt to lash out online as a cry for help or to vent justified frustration. This is your cue to put out the fire by speaking one-on-one with your child, and providing other supportive services.

REACQUAINT YOURSELF WITH THE WORKS OF MARTIN LUTHER KING, NELSON MANDELA, AND MAYA ANGELOU.

We grew up consuming iconic works/ orations, such as "I Have A Dream" (MLK), Long Walk to Freedom (Mandela), and I Know Why the Caged Bird Sings (Angelou). Read these with your children. It's important for young people, especially young African American boys and girls, to understand how these pillars of truth have made positive changes for every race, creed, and color.

THE STORY DOESN'T END HERE...

VISIT
ZUIKERPRESS.COM

... to learn more about Johnathan's story, see behind-the-scenes videos of Johnathan and his family, and learn more about how to overcome **RACISM**.

Our **WEBSITE** is another resource to help our readers deal with the issues that they face every day. Log on to find advice from experts, links to helpful organizations and literature, and more real-life experiences from young people just like you.

Spotlighting young writers with heartfelt stories that enlighten and inspire.

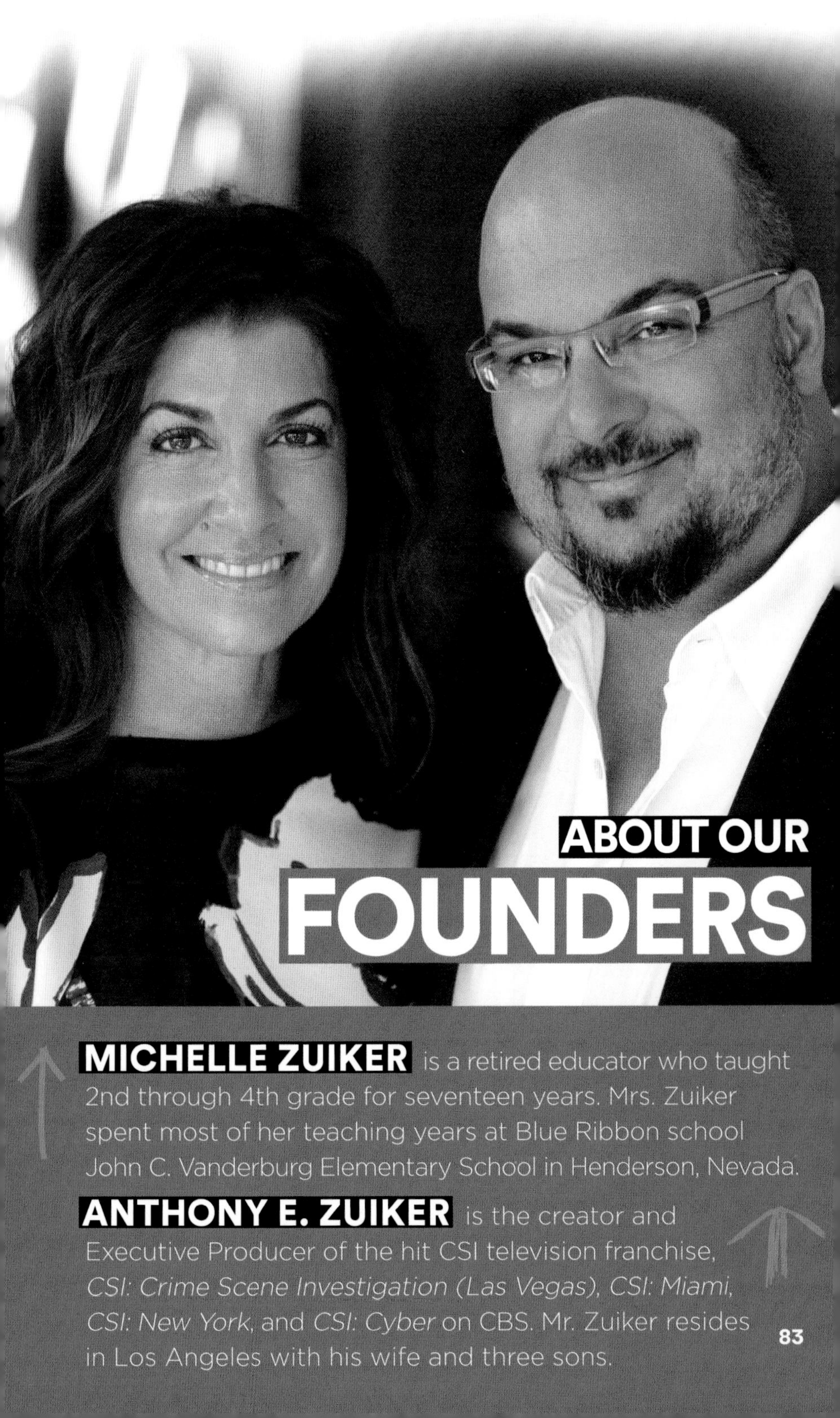

ABOUT OUR FOUNDERS

MICHELLE ZUIKER is a retired educator who taught 2nd through 4th grade for seventeen years. Mrs. Zuiker spent most of her teaching years at Blue Ribbon school John C. Vanderburg Elementary School in Henderson, Nevada.

ANTHONY E. ZUIKER is the creator and Executive Producer of the hit CSI television franchise, *CSI: Crime Scene Investigation (Las Vegas)*, *CSI: Miami*, *CSI: New York*, and *CSI: Cyber* on CBS. Mr. Zuiker resides in Los Angeles with his wife and three sons.

ABOUT OUR
ILLUSTRATORS
& EDITOR...

DON HUDSON– ILLUSTRATOR

Don Hudson has been a professional artist in Los Angeles for twenty years. He's had the opportunity to work in comics, animation, advertising and even Broadway!

If you want to know more about Don, go to **www.dchudson.blogspot.com**.

GARRY LEACH– COVER ARTIST

is a British artist best known for his work co-creating the new *Marvelman* with writer Alan Moore. As an artist Garry was a frequent contributor to *2000AD* working on *Dan Dare*, *Judge Dredd*, *The V.C.s.* and *Future Shocks*. At DC Comics Garry worked on *Legion of Superheroes*, *Hit Man*, *Monarchy* and *Global Frequency*, while over at Marvel Comics, he inked Chris Weston on *The Twelve*. Garry has been a cover artist for Marvel, DC, *2000AD*, *Eclipse*, *Dynamic Forces*, and Kellogg's Corn Flakes.

FAHRIZA KAMAPUTRA– COLORIST

was born and raised in southern Jakarta. In 2010 he worked as colorist on a local comic book, *Vienetta and the Stupid Aliens,* which led to his work on the web comic *Rokki,* and Madeleine Holly-Rosling's *Boston Metaphysical Society* with the studio STELLAR LABS. Fahriza now works as a freelance artist.

DAVE ELLIOTT–EDITOR

has more than thirty-five years of experience working and garnering awards in every aspect of the entertainment industry, from writer and artist, to editor and publisher. Dave has worked on diverse titles such as *A1, Deadline, Viz Comic, Heavy Metal* magazine, *2000AD, Justice League of America, Transformers, GI Joe,* the *Real Ghostbusters* and *Doctor Who.* He also developed projects for Johnny Depp, Dwayne Johnson, and Tom Cruise. Through his own company, AtomekArt, Dave has created his own graphic novel series, *Odyssey* and *The Weirding Willows.*

85

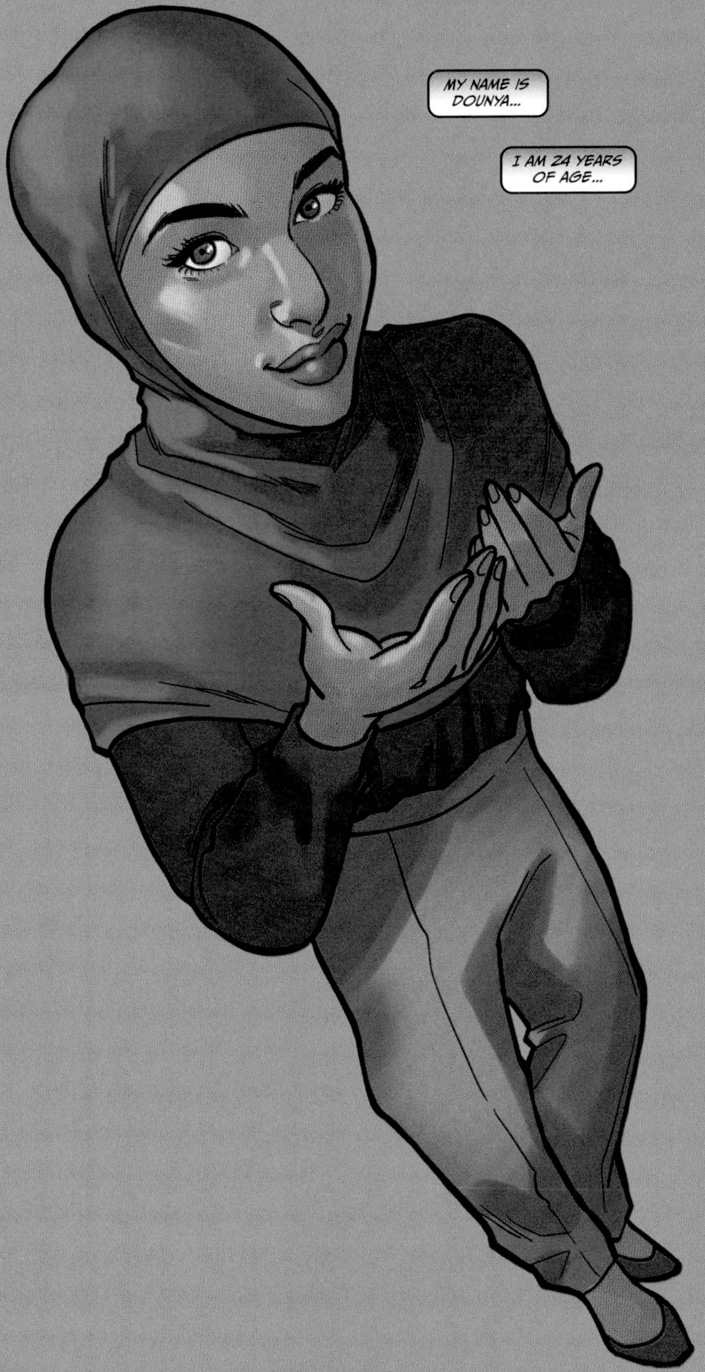
MY NAME IS DOUNYA...
I AM 24 YEARS OF AGE...

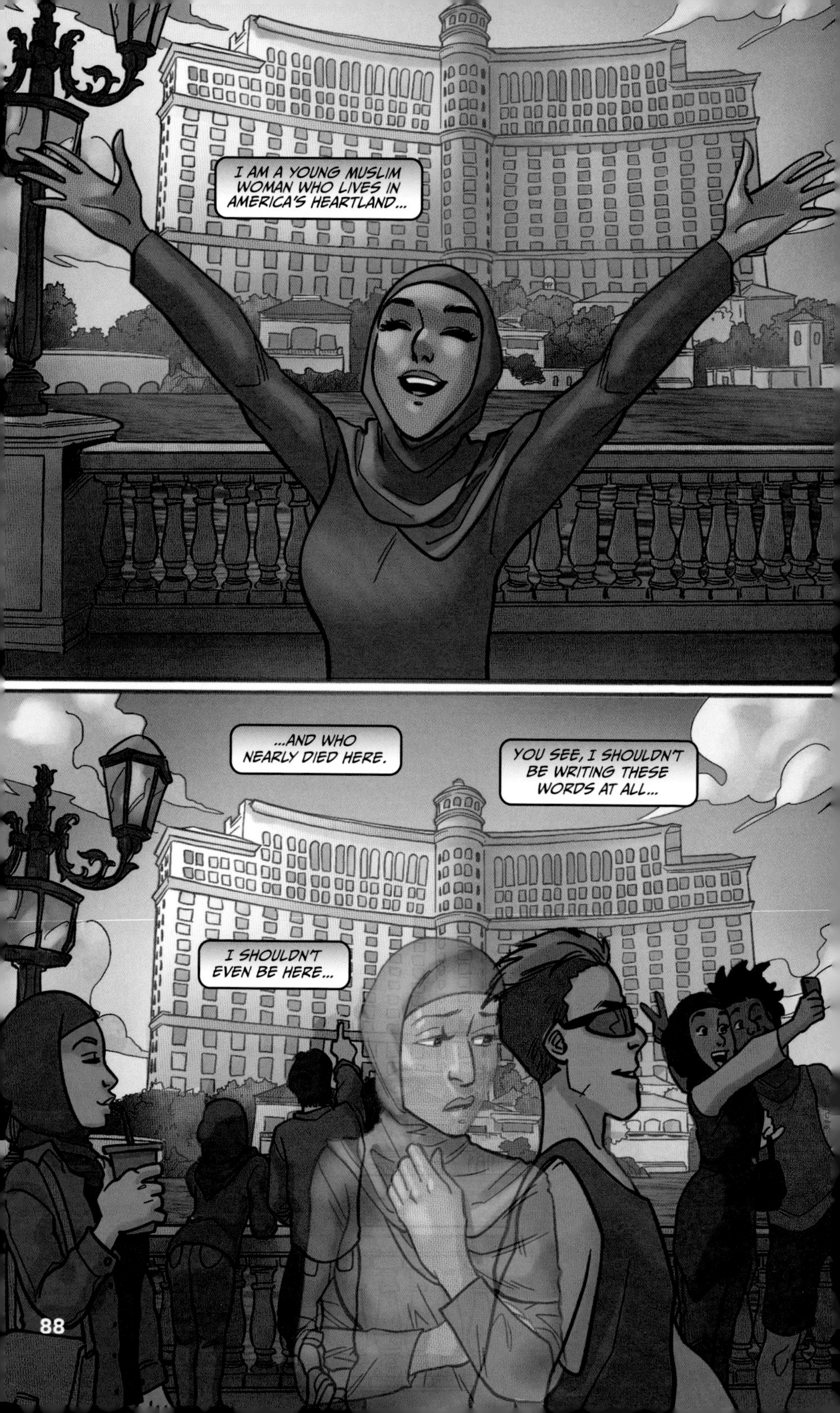
I AM A YOUNG MUSLIM WOMAN WHO LIVES IN AMERICA'S HEARTLAND...
...AND WHO NEARLY DIED HERE.
YOU SEE, I SHOULDN'T BE WRITING THESE WORDS AT ALL...
I SHOULDN'T EVEN BE HERE...

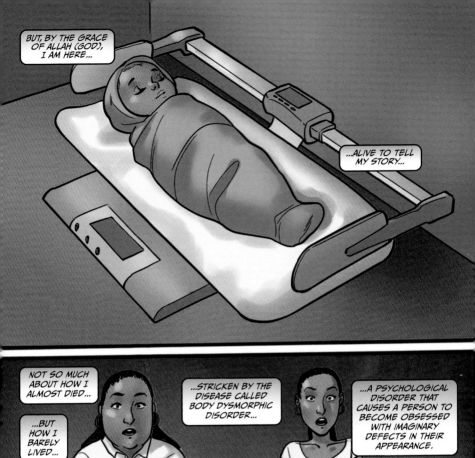

BUT, BY THE GRACE OF ALLAH (GOD), I AM HERE...

...ALIVE TO TELL MY STORY...

NOT SO MUCH ABOUT HOW I ALMOST DIED...

...BUT HOW I BARELY LIVED...

...STRICKEN BY THE DISEASE CALLED BODY DYSMORPHIC DISORDER...

...A PSYCHOLOGICAL DISORDER THAT CAUSES A PERSON TO BECOME OBSESSED WITH IMAGINARY DEFECTS IN THEIR APPEARANCE.

89

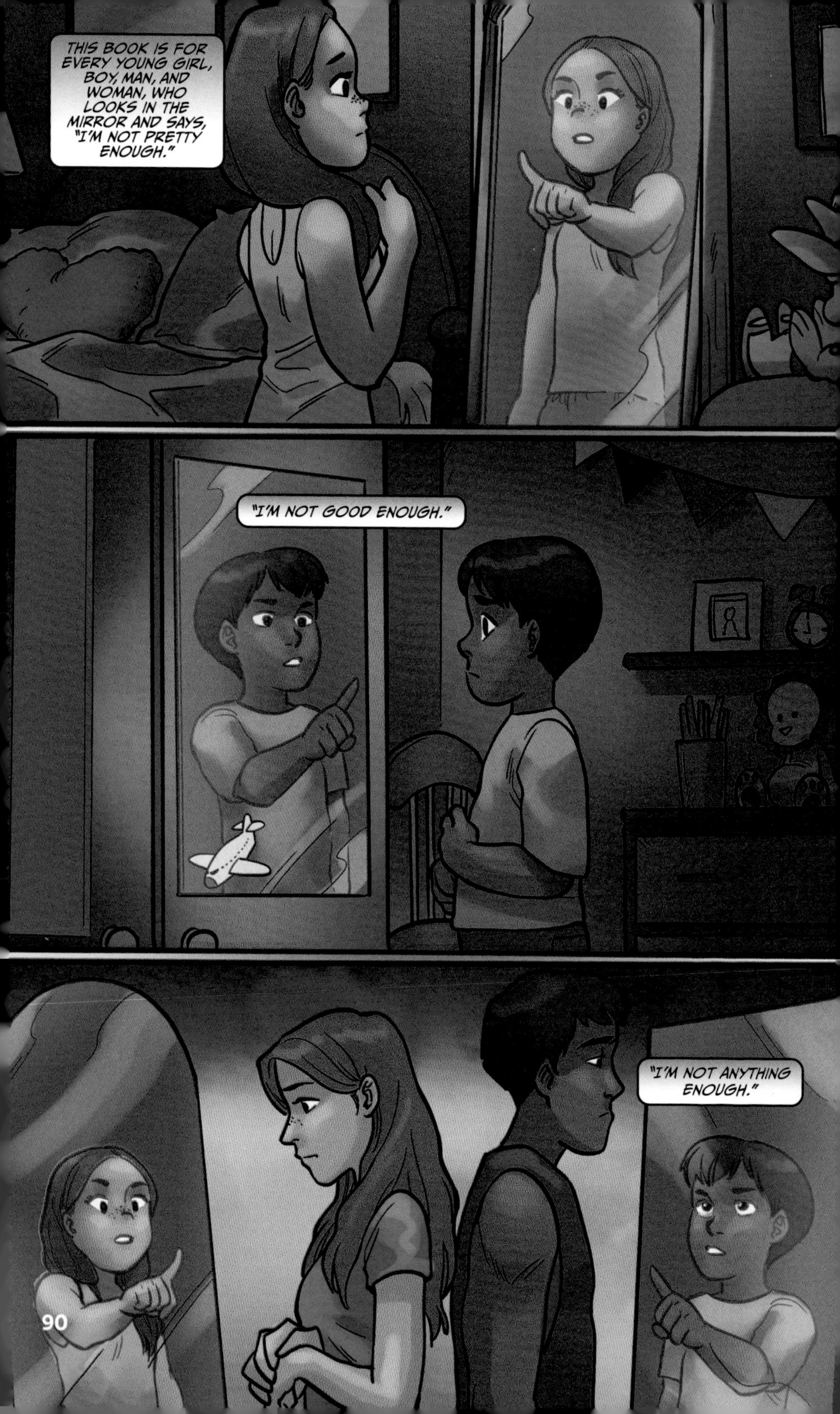
THIS BOOK IS FOR EVERY YOUNG GIRL, BOY, MAN, AND WOMAN, WHO LOOKS IN THE MIRROR AND SAYS, "I'M NOT PRETTY ENOUGH."
"I'M NOT GOOD ENOUGH."
"I'M NOT ANYTHING ENOUGH."

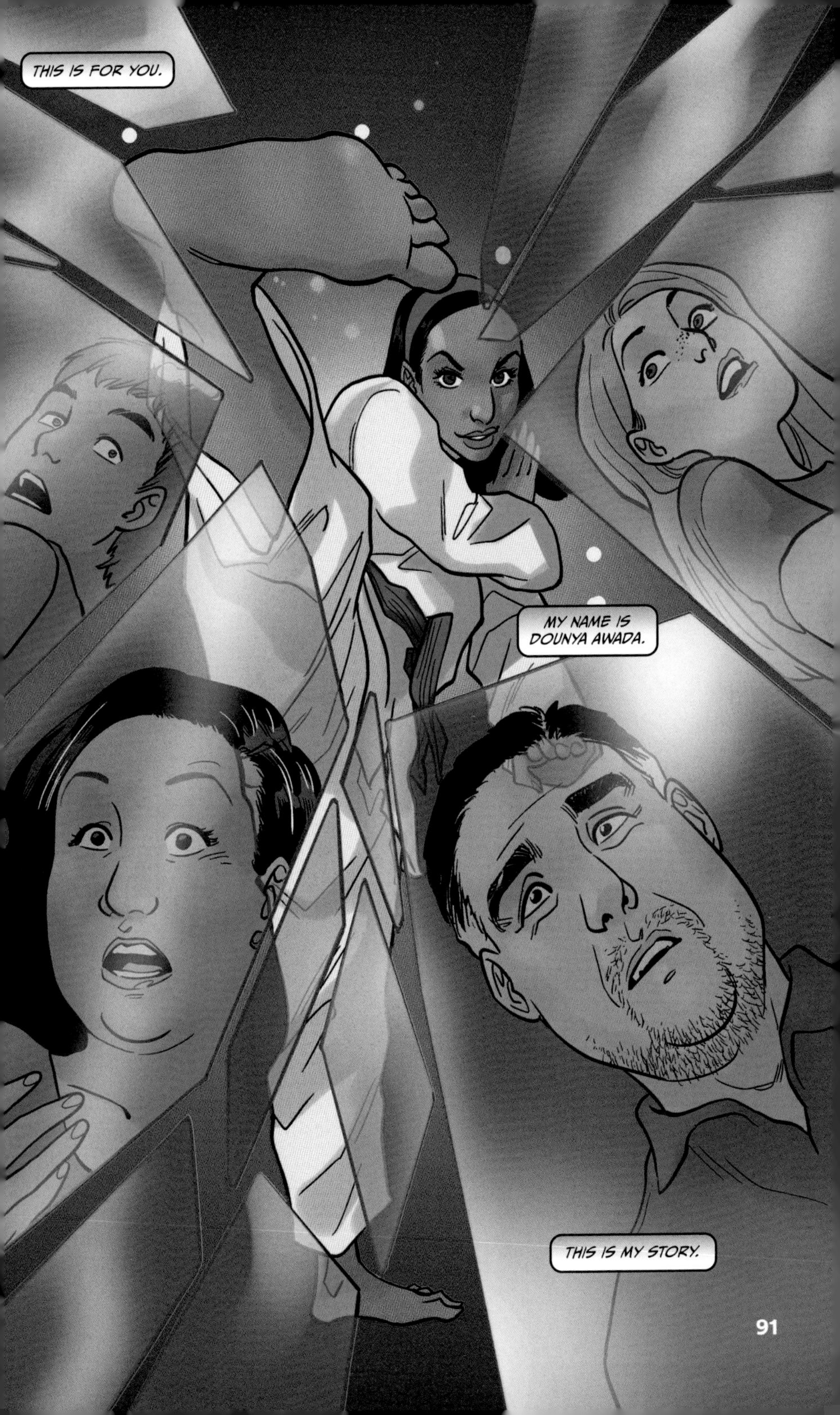
THIS IS FOR YOU.
MY NAME IS DOUNYA AWADA.
THIS IS MY STORY.

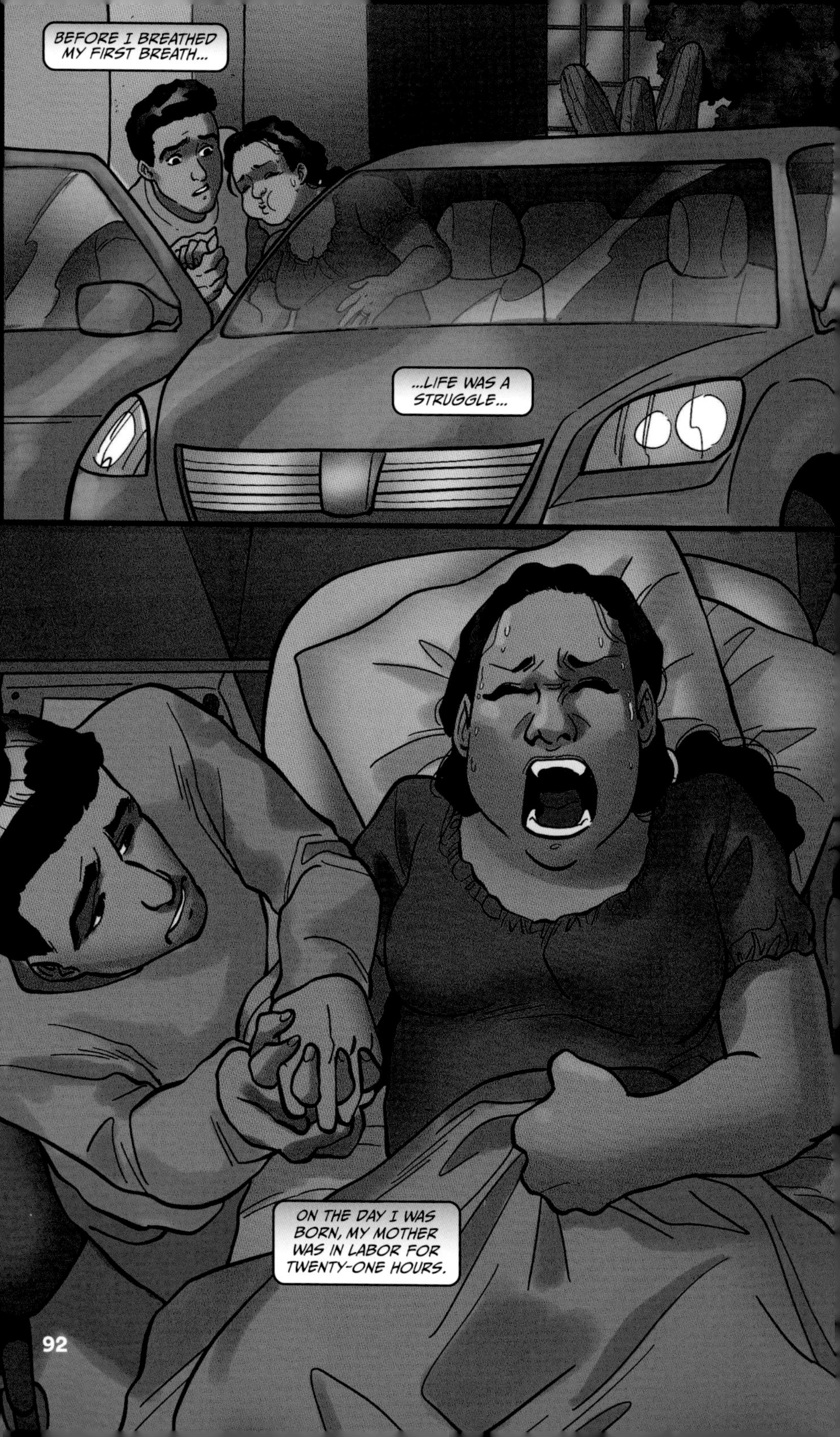
BEFORE I BREATHED MY FIRST BREATH...
...LIFE WAS A STRUGGLE...
ON THE DAY I WAS BORN, MY MOTHER WAS IN LABOR FOR TWENTY-ONE HOURS.

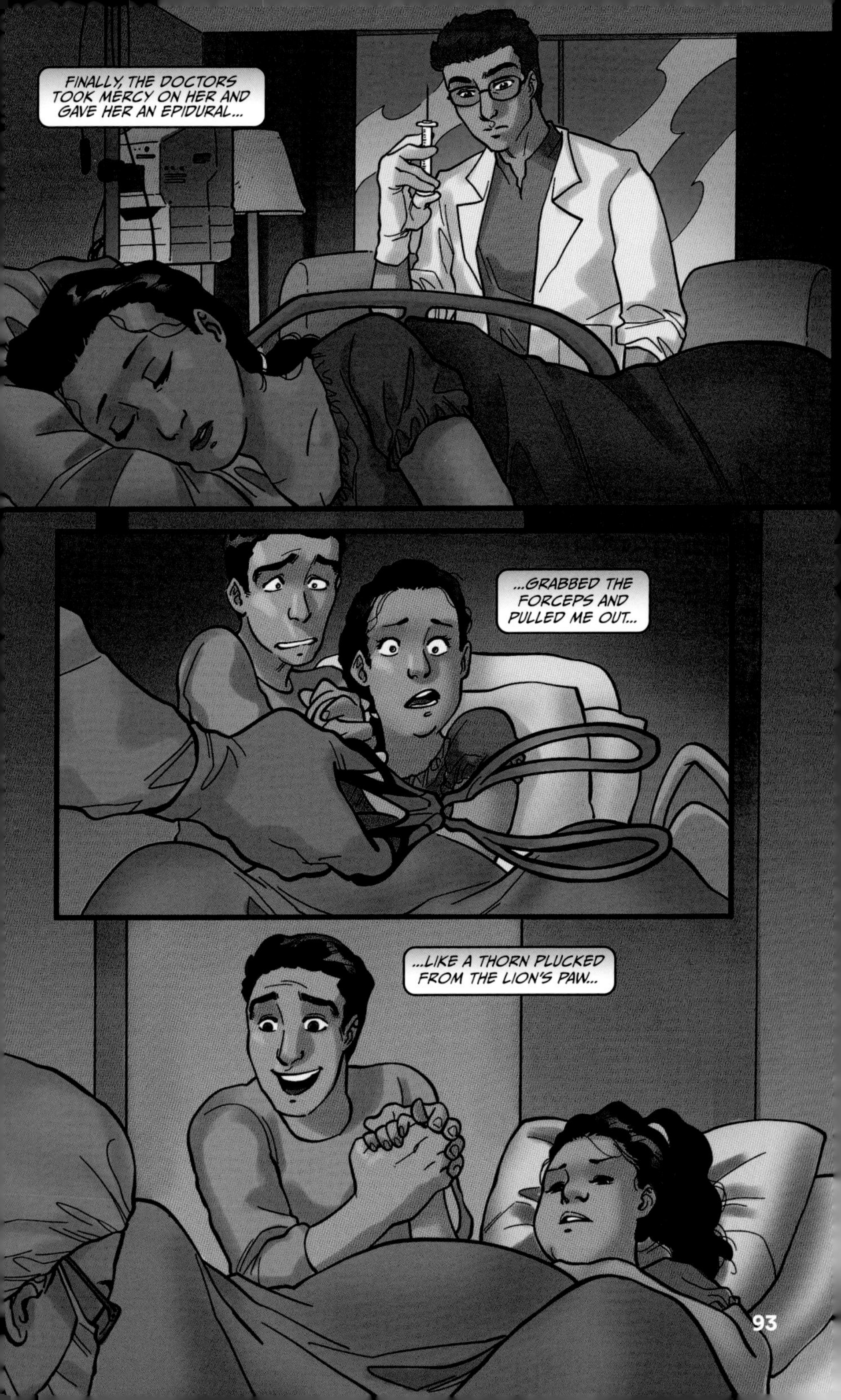
FINALLY, THE DOCTORS TOOK MERCY ON HER AND GAVE HER AN EPIDURAL...
...GRABBED THE FORCEPS AND PULLED ME OUT...
...LIKE A THORN PLUCKED FROM THE LION'S PAW...

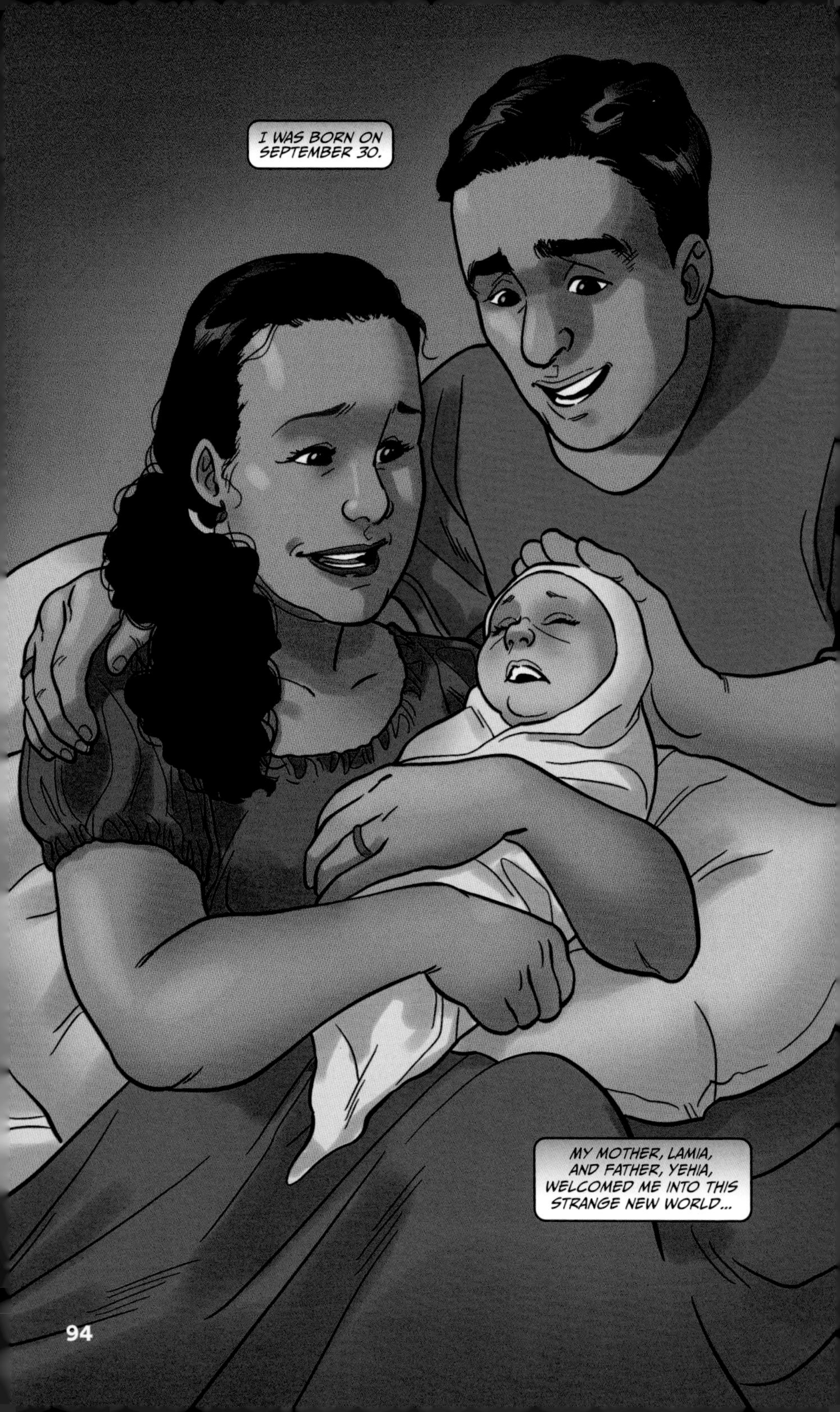
I WAS BORN ON SEPTEMBER 30.
MY MOTHER, LAMIA, AND FATHER, YEHIA, WELCOMED ME INTO THIS STRANGE NEW WORLD...

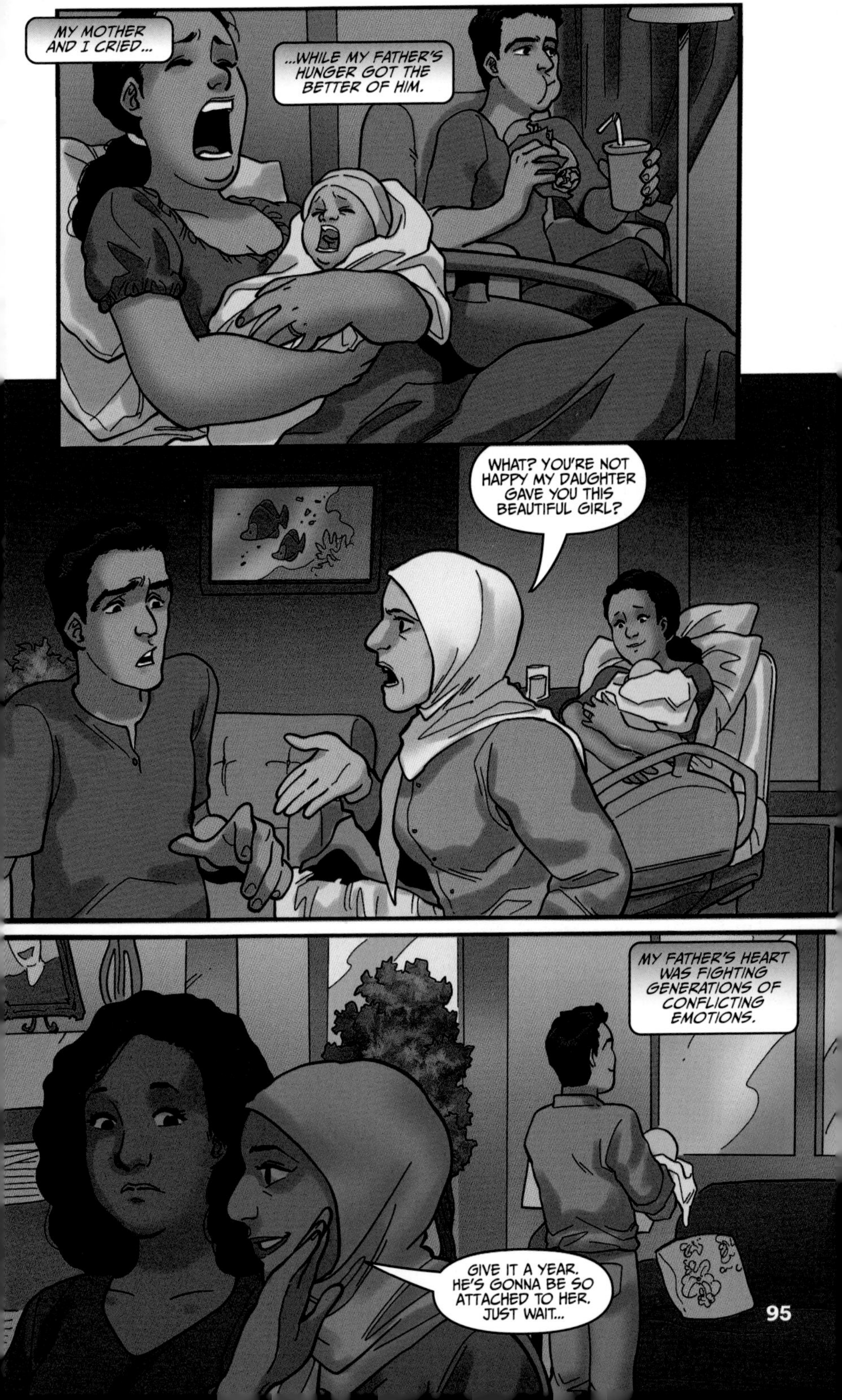
MY MOTHER AND I CRIED...
...WHILE MY FATHER'S HUNGER GOT THE BETTER OF HIM.
WHAT? YOU'RE NOT HAPPY MY DAUGHTER GAVE YOU THIS BEAUTIFUL GIRL?
MY FATHER'S HEART WAS FIGHTING GENERATIONS OF CONFLICTING EMOTIONS.
GIVE IT A YEAR. HE'S GONNA BE SO ATTACHED TO HER. JUST WAIT...

NEW FOR SPRING 2019

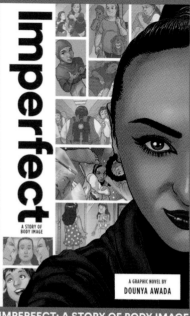

IMPERFECT: A STORY OF BODY IMAGE

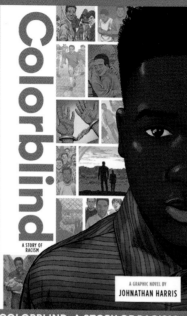

COLORBLIND: A STORY OF RACISM

COMING FALL 2019

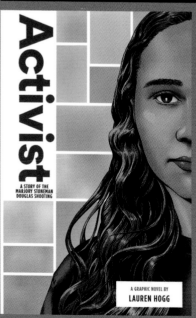

ACTIVIST: A STORY OF THE MARJORY STONEMAN DOUGLAS SHOOTING

IDENTITY: A STORY OF TRANSITIONING